Broadway Christian Church Fort Wayne
Thriving As a Working Woman   CL14 Ell
Ellis, Gwen

0000   4472

P9-EMH-232

Thriving As a Working Woman

EXCLUSIVE CHRISTIAN FAMILY BOOK CLUB EDITION

Thriving
AS A
WORKING WOMAN

GWEN ELLIS

COMPLETE AND UNABRIDGED

CHRISTIAN Family BOOK CLUB

Since 1948, The Book Club You Can Trust

Other books by Gwen Ellis Weising
Raising Kids on Purpose for the Fun of It
Finding Time for Family Fun
Finding Dollars for Family Fun
Eve: God's Word for Women Today
A Working Woman's Guide to Joy

© 1995 by Gwen Ellis
All rights reserved
Cover illustration copyright © 1994 by Tim Stout.

Scripture taken from the *New American Standard Bible,* © 1960, 1962, 1963, 1968, 1971, 1972, 1973, 1975, 1977 by The Lockman Foundation. Used by permission.

Library of Congress Cataloging-in-Publication Data

Ellis, Gwen.
   Thriving as a working woman / Gwen Ellis.
      p.   cm.
   Includes bibliographical references.
   ISBN 0-8423-4598-1 (pbk.)
   1. Women—Employment.   2. Women—Life skills guides.   I. Title.
HD6053.W43   1995
650.1'082—dc20   94-42377

Printed in the United States of America

00   99   98   97   96   95
 9   8   7   6   5   4   3   2

First hardcover edition for Christian Family Book Club: 1997

This book is dedicated in general to working women everywhere and in particular to those very busy women who took the time to answer my survey, often filling it out between the multiple tasks that fill up a working woman's life. Some of those women even thanked me for the opportunity to participate in the survey. I am humbled by their willingness to help. Thanks!

CONTENTS

PREFACE

Dear working friend,

It is my deepest hope that something in this book will make your life a little easier, a little happier, a little more meaningful. We—you and I—have so much to contribute to the world. We have so much passion for life.

You have been my passion for several years now. I realize working women are struggling. I realize life is not always easy for most of you, who have two full-time jobs. I realize friendships are difficult with the schedule you keep and that you often feel isolated and alone.

Lest you think I'm some kind of expert on the subjects about which I've written, let me assure you I'm not. I'm struggling just like you are. I sometimes feel inadequate for the task God has called me to. I get weary and wonder what life is all about. I too have to work with a variety of personalities in the office. I get tired of systems that don't work, just like you do.

But I've learned from writing this book. I've learned about rest and the importance of keeping a strong spiritual life. I've learned it's important to ask for help when I need it. I've learned, because I've done it, how to find a job that fits me.

I trust that you too will find something—even one or two nuggets—to help you live your life a little better, a little richer, with more love, friendship, and companionship.

ACKNOWLEDGMENTS

My deepest gratitude goes first to LaVonne Neff, who heard me mention this project at a writers conference and approached me about doing it for Tyndale House. Her guidance and helpfulness are deeply appreciated.

Thanks to Ken Petersen, who picked up the ball when LaVonne returned to school. Thanks for your enthusiasm.

Thanks to Tyndale House for making me a part of your family while writing this book. The surprise packages and greetings that arrived several times during the year were a great encouragement to me. Thanks to my editor, Kathy Stinnette, who, from the first contact, made me feel I'm an important part of her life.

Thanks to Mary Whelchel, who has led the way in encouraging Christian working women. Thanks, Mary, for the times we talked and the encouragement you gave me in practical ways.

Thanks, most of all, to the many who have shown all of us who must work what it means to be a Christian working woman.

INTRODUCTION

Sandra came home from an eight-hour job and a one-hour commute to the aroma of dinner cooking. The kids were busy with homework. Someone had thought to set the table, and there was even a centerpiece of flowers. It was wonderful—but it hadn't always been this way.

She remembered coming home from work one day a few months ago, finding chaos, and realizing it was the norm. That was when she'd decided something had to change. She had felt angry with these people she loved. She had felt they had no gratitude and that she was only their servant. She knew her attitude was unhealthy and destructive to her family and to herself, so she started that night to determine what could be done.

She began by asking herself some questions:

- Why was she working?
- Was it necessary for her to work outside the home?
- Were her standards too high? not high enough?
- Did her family understand what was expected of them?
- What rewards were they getting when they met her expectations?

The change didn't happen overnight. It took a lot of soul-searching on Sandra's part to understand, first, that she had choices and, second, that a big part of the problem was her inability to communicate what needed to be done around the home.

There are two kinds of working women: those who work because they want to and those who work because they must. The category into which you fall matters little for the scope of this book; all working women have similar joys and struggles — too much to do, not enough time to do it in.

You *can* succeed in the dual role of employee and homemaker. You (and your family if you have one) can benefit from your working. You can grow as a person through paid employment, whether you see it as a long-term career or a short-term job. But to succeed in making your home life and your work life pleasant, you need to learn how to prioritize, plan, and think through your options. You need resources — lots of them — and that's what this book is about.

In the pages of this book you will find ideas for enjoying — not just enduring — your life; not just coping as a working woman, but succeeding with style. The ideas come from many sources — even some from women like yourself.

My deepest wish is that something written here will give you new insights about the joys that can be yours as a working woman.

PART
ONE

Finding
a Way to Thrive

CHAPTER 1

The Things That Try My Soul

Up at dawn. Dressed and on the road in the morning rush. In flight to Seattle, Anchorage, Fairbanks and back nearly twelve hours later — Alaska Airlines flight attendant Kelli Wike lives life at a supersonic pace.

One day, driving her toddler, Karli, to the baby-sitter's house, the fast track caught up with her. Karli threw up. Wike cleaned up as best she could and raced for the sitter's and the airport.

Stopping at the bathroom, glancing in the mirror, it hit her: "I saw bags under my eyes, my skin didn't have the glow it usually does. I just saw myself looking older, more ragged. . . . "[1]

Kelli Wike is just one of the women who feel that way — ragged, worn around the edges from trying to live two hectic lives at the same time, and constantly feeling guilty about being a working mother. Many of us have painted ourselves into a tight corner by thinking we could have it all.

Some women are recounting the cost to themselves and their families and are making changes by cutting down on the

A survival tip I got from one of my college profs: Keep an "encouragement file." Place in it encouraging notes from others, mementos, uplifting quotes, etc.—anything that will remind you of your value and worth at times when you feel worthless or unappreciated.

—Carla

time spent in their paid employment. Some are even cutting out their jobs altogether and making do with less money. But some must continue to work, and others *want* to work outside their homes.

It *is* possible to work full-time and be a homemaker—and do them both successfully. We all know women who have managed both. Their kids grow up to be fine, their homes are clean enough, and they feel fulfilled in a way homemaking alone would not have provided for them.

But over and over women identify the same basic problem areas, the things that try their souls. They take slightly different slants for various groups of women—the mother of small children, the never-married single, the working woman with no children at home, and the divorced or widowed starting-over-again woman —but the basic problems are the same. Let's take a look at some of them.

TIME MANAGEMENT

In a recent survey, working women said their *number one problem* is time management. Many women work a forty-hour week for an employer and then put in another twenty or thirty hours of housework and child care. The result is overtired, cranky moms whose frustration spills all over their families.

PRIORITIES

Other surveyed women said they have trouble establishing priorities. With so many demands on their time, they are having trouble discerning what is most important. Often the reason they have trouble prioritizing their activities and creating a livable time schedule is that they have never established goals for their lives. These women do not know what is important in their lives, so the urgent (but unimportant) gets first priority. The result is a nagging dissatisfaction with life, a gnawing feeling of life passing by and of never having done what really matters most to them.

FINANCES

Some women said managing their finances is a big problem. Some are working to provide the basic essentials for their children; some to buy a house; some to provide extras for the family; some to provide an education for their children. Whatever their reasons for working, many women felt that the more they work and the more money they earn, the more they need.

These women want to learn how to budget, to spend wisely, to become savers. Others want investment information, information about retirement savings plans, IRAs, and Keogh plans. A few, who've been able to accumulate a little capital, want to learn about stocks, bonds, and mutual funds.

NEED FOR CHRISTIAN FELLOWSHIP

Some felt the need to establish friendships with other Christian working women but truly don't have the time to do so. They longed for early morning or evening support groups in which they could network with other working women. Some even expressed a desire for a pen pal—someone in like circumstances with whom to correspond.

DIFFICULT BOSSES
Many of the women surveyed expressed frustration with their work situations. Some had bosses who were abrasive, abusive, difficult, and dishonest and who displayed a host of other negative attributes.

COWORKERS
Some had problems with coworkers. Office jealousies were a problem. Some felt harassed by fellow workers. Others wanted to know how to receive more recognition on the job.

LOW SELF-ESTEEM
After all that has been written on the subject of self-esteem, numbers of women expressed a continuing struggle with it. They realized their low self-esteem was affecting relationships both on and off the job. One woman said, "I want to know how to establish and maintain my individuality and not be swallowed by the system."

WORKPLACE CONFLICTS
Some women were angry and didn't know how to let go of their anger. Some felt insecure in their positions at work. Others needed help in avoiding or recovering from burnout.

NEED FOR CAREER GUIDANCE

Some talked about the need for help with resume preparation and knowing where the best jobs are. One woman was concerned about aging and what would happen to her in her chosen occupation as she gets older.

LACK OF PERSONAL SUPPORT

Over and over women expressed a need for a little tenderness, caring, and pampering. They wanted a housekeeper or someone to help out at home. Many expressed in their own words what I've always believed: What every working woman needs is a "wife."

HEALTH

Still others admitted they are not adequately taking care of their own health. They want simple, inexpensive exercise programs and healthful, easy-to-cook recipes. They realized stress is taking a big toll on their lives and that they must do something about it or pay the consequences.

PARENTING

Many worried about their role as a working mother. They expressed guilt over not spending enough quality time with their children. They wanted to know how to balance motherhood and career. Single mothers needed to know how to order their priorities to best meet their children's needs.

TWO-CAREER FAMILIES

Married working women expressed a need for better relationships both with their children and with their husbands.

They wanted to know how other families divide the labor in a two-career situation.

SINGLE WORKING WOMEN

Single working women wanted help coping with the loneliness that assails them when they go home. They needed to know how to handle office relationships, especially those involving sexual harassment and jealousies.

Single mothers were the ones who expressed the most need of all. How does a single mother cope with being a full-time career woman and the only parent in residence?

YOU'RE NOT ALONE

Throughout all of the survey responses ran some common threads—words like *coping, wisdom, peace, relaxation, understanding, resolution, strength,* and *personal growth.* These are a good indication of the needs of working women.

If any of the above concerns are yours, be assured you are not alone. You are part of a great company of working women who feel as you do. We are a sisterhood of employed women who want to find answers to the problems today's lifestyle creates.

In the pages of this book you will find ideas, hope, understanding of your needs, and resources to help you thrive as a working woman. Now let's begin with some basics.

WHY ARE YOU WORKING?

All women work, but some have chosen to be employed for pay, and their work is outside their homes. Of those who have chosen to be employed, there are two kinds: those who *want* to work and those who *must* work.

A friend told me of an ongoing war being waged over the lines of Prodigy, the on-line, subscriber computer service. One of the services of Prodigy is a bulletin board, where individuals can post notices. If you are trying to buy or sell something, locate an old recipe, or get any other kind of information, you can let everyone know through the bulletin board and then wait for responses.

Michelle began to read what women were saying to each other about working through these bulletins. It was explosive. Women not employed outside their homes were asking those who were why they worked. The nonemployed women thought the employed women should be home with their children. The employed women were responding, vociferously, that they have no choice. Money was the issue, and they really would rather be home with the kids!

In a recent survey by a Connecticut-based firm, working women were asked what would make them stop working. In 1987, 35 percent said they would stop if they had enough money. But by 1990, 56 percent said they would stop for the same reason. That's an 18 percent change in three years, and it shows that women are working mostly because they need money. Fifty-six percent of women who work would rather not be working at all.[2] The need for money is a real issue. The high cost of real estate

*F*lowers on my desk or some sort of personal statement of beauty, such as a basket of shells, help me thrive during the work day. —*Candy*

in many parts of the country makes two incomes a necessity if many couples are ever to have their own home.

Most parents want their children to go to college, and college costs have escalated until they almost reach the stratosphere. Although children can and should help earn their way through college, there is a limit to the amount of time they can work and still do an adequate job with their studies. A college professor friend of mine recently said with a sigh, "The students are different than they used to be. They are less motivated to study, less goal oriented, less ambitious. Of course," she said, "many of them work twenty-five to thirty hours a week just to stay in school. They are too tired to study when the time comes." If a student works too many hours just to stay in school and is too tired to learn, it defeats the whole purpose of going to school, and the family is throwing away massive amounts of money. The only solution is for him to get help either through loans or from his parents—and that usually means Mom has to work to help out.

Some women work because they feel they have a God-given mission to fulfill in life. They are doctors, teachers, missionaries, and social workers. Deep within them is a need to perform a service for humanity.

There are other women who work just because they enjoy working, and there are those who work because they have too much time on their hands. They would rather be making a positive contribution to society through a job than looking for something to do at home.

A LOOK AT HISTORY
Whatever the reason, about 65 percent of all women are

now employed outside their homes. The majority of small businesses begun today are started by women. Women are doing everything from heading corporations to construction work. They are in every part of the workforce.

Women have always worked and worked hard. For thousands of years they have worked with men in the fields to plant and bring in crops. They've made soap by hand, sheared sheep, and then carded and spun the wool into yarn. They've made fabric; tended huge gardens; picked, canned, and preserved the produce; and borne a child a year. In many parts of the world, women continue to fill these challenging roles.

When industrialization came to America, women began working in factories, where they were grossly underpaid. In many cases their children were considered dispensable and so were put to work in the most dangerous places in the factory.

When the floodgates of immigration opened through such places as Ellis Island, cheap labor poured into America. Some of the cheapest was that of women and children. Some worked in factories, but others did piecework out of their homes, such as gluing the linings in shoes and sewing on buttons, for pennies per unit.

Later, women began to be employed primarily in what were considered "acceptable" jobs for them. They worked as teachers, nurses, and secretaries. With the advent of World War II, women again went to work in factories — and other "men's" jobs — to support the war effort. Not until recently have women begun to enter nontraditional fields as a matter of course: those of police officers, firefighters, heavy equipment operators, pilots, and many others.

T make clear distinctions between work and play—and whatever I do, I do it fully. If I'm writing, I immerse myself in thinking of nothing but expressing myself on paper. If I'm editing, I think only of eagle eyes and catching every pesky mistake.

— *Lynn*

Not long ago I was traveling by car and stopped at a service station. In the rest room I met a woman dressed in heavy boots, a rough wool shirt, a heavy coat, leather gloves, a hard hat, and a neon orange bib. It was obviously she was working on the road construction crew I'd passed on the highway. As she washed her hands, she turned to me and said, "Ah, hot water. That feels so good. I get so dirty."

"Aha!" I said. "Under all that masculine garb beats a very feminine heart."

"Yes." She smiled and continued, "I have to work to help my children through school, and this pays better than anything else I can do."

It really is not new for women to work outside their homes. What is new, however, is the higher percentage of working women and the kinds of roles these working women are filling.

WHY DO YOU WORK?

Since working can be both a positive and negative experience and since some women have the option of working or not working, we need to take a serious look at why we have chosen to be employed outside our homes. If we never seriously consider why we are working, we may also fail to consider whether this is the right job, the best job for our circumstances.

Here is a quiz to help you focus on your purposes for working:

- Am I fulfilling a mission or personal calling through my work?
- Does working build my self-esteem?
- Do I have the support of my family?
- Have I dealt with the division of labor in our home?
- After expenses, how much am I actually making?
- Are we saving a portion of what I make or spending it all to raise our standard of living?
- Do we really need the things we're buying with the money I earn?
- Is there another way to meet those needs?
- Are we eating out more because I'm too tired to cook?
- Are we buying more services?
- Could we get by with one car (or without a car) if I were not working?
- Do I need more clothes because I am working?
- How is my working impacting my family?
- How is my working impacting my health?
- Is the profit margin worth it?

When I went back to work after having children, I had two goals. My long-range goal was to help my children through college, but my immediate goal was making enough money to take a family vacation in Europe. We felt the educational experience the kids would gain on such a trip was worth the cost. By my working a full year and saving every penny I made, we were able to take that trip.

Although my goals in the beginning were purely monetary, I discovered working had some side benefits I had not counted on. Working enhanced my sense of self-worth, as I found I was good at managing people, developing products, creating programs, and a lot of other things.

You too may decide to work not out of necessity but to provide some pleasurable experience for your family, or because you enjoy working, or because working gives you a place to learn, stretch, and grow. Those are valid reasons for being employed.

We're not here to judge motives. We are here to say, please consider why you're working and measure the value of your earnings against the problems, time constrictions, stresses, and added expenses that you will incur because of your work. If, as the mother of young children, you have the option to work or not work, then seriously consider what your working will do to your children. Pray about your decision, and then do what you think best.

What Is Your Frustration Level?

There's a lot written about frustration because there is a lot of frustration to write about. In her book *The Twenty-Five-Hour Woman*, Sybil Stanton quotes Dr. Hans Selye, who says that frustration and indecision are the most harmful psychogenic stressors and maintains that "neither uninhibited successful work nor even final hopeless defeat . . . is as demanding as the destructive effect of unresolved contradictory efforts."[3]

Frustration! The aggravation of being pulled in two directions or not being able to resolve complex or even not-so-complex situations. The end result can be very destructive to us.

If our lives are constantly filled with a deep sense of frustration, we are jeopardizing our health, our relationships, and even our work. It is imperative that we find the source of our frustration and deal with it. For some, finding a support group may help to deal with it. For others it may require a job change, training, or retraining. For others it may even require the assistance of a professional counselor to get at the underlying causes of frustration.

Are you frustrated? What is it that frustrates you? No, I don't mean the surface things. What is really at the bottom of your frustration?

Here's an evaluation quiz to help you analyze your frustration level. Answer true or false.

- I have more problems than other people. **T/F**
- My problems are more severe than other people's problems. **T/F**
- I get very angry when I think about how difficult my life is. **T/F**
- I often find myself thinking, *If only I had more education [training, money, beauty, charm], then I could truly succeed.* **T/F**
- I am often angry with my spouse/children because they don't help me enough. **T/F**

- I try and try to please my boss, but I never feel like I do. I don't know what else to do. **T/F**
- My boss has no understanding of how much work I have to do, but just keeps piling it on. **T/F**
- I want to do a good job at work, but there are conditions that keep me from it. **T/F**
- Sometimes I'm given tasks to do for which I have had no training. I hate feeling like I'm doing an inferior job because of lack of training. **T/F**

If you answered *true* to seven or more statements, you are highly frustrated and are headed for a crash.

If five to six statements are true for you, you have some frustration, which should be dealt with before it becomes more severe.

If you answered zero to four true, you are probably experiencing normal work-related frustration. However, don't ignore the problem areas. They have a way of snow-balling until you may become extremely frustrated.

SUPERWOMAN YOU'RE NOT
You may think you're Superwoman and can do it all. You may convince everyone else and even yourself that you are, but that doesn't make it so. There haven't been any super-women created in quite a long time.

I once thought I was. I worked full-time, wrote books, took care of the house and yard, made the major family purchases, taught in the church, sang in a couple of choirs, sewed, did handiwork, etc. It used to be a joke around our office about how many things I could do at the same time.

People used to tell me how tired I looked, and I thought it was some kind of badge of honor.

I guess I'm pretty tough. It took some time for the crash to come, but when it did, it was huge. I wore out on all sides all at once. I became so numb from overwork that I could no longer sort out my life.

I've learned that I am *not* Superwoman. And now that I've made that admission, I find that I no longer want to be. I'm still involved in a lot of activities, but I'm not trying so hard to prove who I am by my work. I'm motivated by a different set of values than I once was.

Most of us have a limit as to how much we can do and still thrive. Realistically assessing what you can do without becoming frustrated, burning out, or costing your family a huge price will lend longevity, contentment, and joy to your working life more than anything else you can do.

What is realistic for us as working women? Each woman must decide for herself—but she must consciously decide. Choosing to ignore the issue is in itself a decision—a decision to let circumstances manage us instead of our being able to manage them.

In this book we'll help you look at your circumstances and make appropriate decisions to enable you to thrive as a working woman. We'll look at problem areas for working women and offer resources and ideas for solving those problems. And throughout, we'll be sharing suggestions and comments from other working women who have learned to thrive.

I use soothing colors and photos of my children to make my office a pleasant place.

—*Kathleen*

SUGGESTED READING

Ruth Klein, *Where Did the Time Go? The Working Woman's Guide to Time Management* (Rocklin, Calif.: Prima, 1992).

Martha Nelson, *The Christian Woman in the Working World* (Nashville: Broadman, 1970).

PROPERTY OF
BROADWAY CHRISTIAN CHURCH LIBRARY
910 BROADWAY
FORT WAYNE, IN 46802

CHAPTER 2

It Takes Planning

In an average lifetime, an American works 70,696 hours . . . sleeps 24 years . . . spends a year looking for misplaced items. Business meetings take up 3 years and commuting takes up 10 months. . . .[1]

I don't have time to think!" Have you ever said it? Ever thought it? Many women feel that way—that they don't have time to think. But if you could stop to think about it, you would soon realize there doesn't seem to be any good reason why we are so busy. We have more convenience foods, quick services, labor-saving devices, automated machines, and instant everything than ever before in history, and yet we have less time. And less time means less time to think.

In a recent article in *Parade* magazine, Ralph Keyes talked about this very problem. He says:

"Our studies clearly show that people feel they have less and less time," reports the Roper poll's Public Pulse. Why should this be? In an age of fax machines and microwave ovens, how did time get so scarce?

*T*here are three deadlines at the office. I plan my tasks around those deadlines. Meeting them keeps me from getting behind and overwhelmed, which then makes me less effective.

—*Sharon*

Shouldn't rising standards of living produce *more* leisure? And can anything be done to alleviate time's pressure?

What we too seldom realize is that modern advantages themselves put pressure on our time. Today's average starter home is twice as big as one built after World War II. That's a lot more house to buy, furnish and maintain.[2]

Keyes is not alone in his thinking. J. B. Schor, in his book *The Overworked American*, says that while we have been gradually developing methods and technologies for reducing our workload (e.g., copy machines, microwave ovens, hair dryers, computers, telephones, and fax machines), we are paradoxically spending more hours working in order to get things done.[3]

In a tongue-in-cheek piece in *Newsweek*, Robert J. Samuelson says,

> Advanced technology enables us to do useful new things or to do old things more efficiently. By contrast, retarded technology creates new and expensive ways of doing things that were once done simply and inexpensively. Worse, it encourages us to do things that don't need doing at all. It has made waste respectable, elaborate, alluring and even fun.[4]

In his article, Keyes lists several factors as contributing to the problem. They are:

- *Too many choices.* We have to take the time to choose between several television programs, cereal brands, friendships, and lots of other things.
- *Time-consuming time-savers.* By simplifying chores, our time-savers encourage us to do more chores. People didn't wash their hair daily in years gone by. Showers and blow-dryers make it possible for them to do so now. Once we let dirt accumulate in inaccessible places. Now we have a vacuum that will suck it out, and so we feel we must.
- *The vanishing pause.* When we used to wind a clock, we had to pause each time we'd turned the handle as far as possible. Now the numbers go sailing by on our electric digital clocks, and if we're not careful, we have to go all the way around again. When we boiled water the old-fashioned way, we had to hang around the kitchen for a few minutes and wait. Now it's ready in two minutes or less in the microwave. Once we had to pause to put a piece of paper in the typewriter, now we don't even pause at the end of the line when keyboarding on the computer.[5]

Those little pauses gave us rest. They gave us breathing space. Maybe it was only snatches of time, but we had moments to think, to reflect.

We pay dearly for all of this speed. We pay with our

bodies, minds, and spirits. Reflection, meditation, and thought processing don't happen on their own. We have to have a plan — not necessarily a time-management plan, but a life plan.

PLAN LIFE

How do we "plan life"? We do it by taking time regularly to ask ourselves, *What is it I truly want out of life?* Then we evaluate all the activities we're engaged (or entrapped) in. Do they truly contribute to our life plan? It takes a lot of personal courage to root out all those activities that only create busyness and detract from the goals that form the purpose of and for our lives.

The lack of a plan for organizing our time is itself a kind of plan. It's a plan to let life run over us, to surrender control over what happens to us to the whims of circumstances and the plans of others. If we have no plan, we will still accomplish a lot, but it won't be in any particular direction. We definitely won't accomplish those things that have the most significance in our lives.

We have to plan life at work and life at home. Some days we need to take a walk during our lunch break for relaxation and exercise. Other days we need to have lunch with a friend. If we have a job where we are on our feet a good portion of our workday, we may need to find a quiet corner and just sit and rest. We need to include in our life plan time for our spouse, children, parents, and friends.

We have to slow down. We have to stop the racing within, but how can we do it? One idea might be to leave your watch at home when you've gone out to play. Ask yourself, *What would be the worst thing that could happen if I don't rush? Can I live with it?* How long has it been since you've lain on your back in the grass and imagined pictures in the clouds? When was the last time you "looked small" at a one-foot patch of earth and tried to see everything that was there? You don't even have to do that much. You can do nothing at all. Sometimes doing nothing is a valid use of your time.

Keyes suggests in his article that we find out where the sanctuaries are near our workplaces or homes. Where are the parks, churches, hotel lobbies, libraries? Sneak into one of these areas during a lunch hour and just listen to life.

YOUR INTERNAL TIME CLOCK

We have to learn to listen to our internal time clock—the clock that makes each of us a morning or night person. Recently I was at a conference where, at breakfast, one of the conferees said to me as he hung down in his oatmeal, "Don't you just feel awful?"

"No, as a matter of fact, I feel great," I chirped. In that moment I realized that I, a morning person, was being disgustingly cheerful to a night person. The night before, he and several other attendees sat up late eating ice cream and laughing and talking. I had slipped out because I was about to turn into a pumpkin, and I didn't think the lively group would appreciate a somnolent author in their midst.

We're all different. Our internal time clocks are set differently, and guess what—it's OK! We just have to learn how to work *with* our bodies and not against them. A basic time management principle is *save prime time for prime projects*. If you know that your very best time of the day is ten o'clock in the morning, then tackle tough jobs at ten o'clock in the morning. If you know you sag in the traces about three in the afternoon, then stay away from working on anything crucial at that time.

My secretary has me figured out very well. Most afternoons she says to me, "It must be about three o'clock. Do you need some coffee, Gwen?" She's spotted my sag time.

BE EFFECTIVE RATHER THAN EFFICIENT

There are some highly effective people who don't care a hoot about efficiency. I think of Annie Dillard, an author who says it takes ten years to write a book. She's not in any hurry. She won the Pulitzer prize at age twenty-nine. At forty-six she has only published eight books. One of her books, *Pilgrim at Tinker Creek,* is a favorite of mine.

Annie took the time to spend endless hours beside Tinker's Creek observing nature. From her observations she shares a totally new way of looking at things. She has proven that it is better to take time, be reflective, think through what to say, and write just one effective book than it is to produce many slipshod manuscripts.

I read about Martin Luther, the great Reformer, who had so much to do he needed to spend three hours in prayer each day just to face it. Was he efficient? I don't know. But I do know he was effective.

Might it be possible to accomplish more by doing less? What if we slowed down, thought out what we were about to do, and counted the cost before we plunged headlong into it? We just can't keep adding activities to our lives. Before we add another "worthwhile endeavor," we need to get rid of something.

We know we can't have it all. But what if we could —

would we want it? Be honest. Would you? What truly brings meaning to your life?

For most of us the answer is family, friends, and our relationship with God. Many of us would also include activities like gardening and sewing, sports, and exercise. If we cut back on our busyness, we'll have time for that which brings meaning to our lives.

What, more than anything else, do you want to do or be? Could you, by cutting back on busyness, find five or ten minutes today to spend on that goal?

BUSYNESS EVALUATION
Use these questions to think about the busyness of your life:

- Would I be more effective if I took more time for myself—time to think, read, and pray?
- Would I be more effective if I took some additional training?
- Should I lower my standard of housekeeping to make room for these pursuits?
- Is there someone living with me that could help me more?
- Are my children involved in the care and maintenance of our home, or am I allowing them to be lazy and not learn how to help?
- Would I be more effective if I

I have always tried to arrange my work schedule, even if it means less pay, so that I get home before the children do. That way I can stay in touch with what's happening at home. —Jan

developed a thoughtful, meditative approach to
life?

- Am I driven by guilt and a need to prove myself?
- Would I be more effective if I were not such a
perfectionist?

KNOWING WHAT TO DO FIRST

All right, you say, *I see the importance of planning as a means of
coping with my life. But where do I start?*

First of all, set aside some quality time for planning. Go
on a retreat. Take a day off work. Get someone to take the
kids for a weekend. It is absolutely essential to quiet ourselves before we can begin to look ahead and see a clear
path to the goals, dreams, and hopes of our lives.

Our goals, dreams, and hopes will be based on what is
truly important in our lives. Our priority planning must
reflect this. Here are some questions to help you think
about priorities:

- Who is/are the most important person(s) in my
life?
- How do I let them know?
- What could I do differently to let them know how
important they are?
- Is my relationship with God important to me?
- How do I show it?
- What changes do I want to make in my religious
life?
- What level of cleanliness do I need to maintain in
my home/yard/car/office to keep me sane?
- What caused me to set this level? Is it realistic?

- What do I expect from my children?
- Am I demanding perfection from imperfect people?
- If so, why? What is behind my demand for perfection?
- What about myself? Do I expect more from myself than I am capable of?
- Do I like myself?
- How do I want to change?

Once you've thought about these questions, you can finally get down to the actual planning. On a big piece of paper, list all the things you want to do before you die. Think widely. Dream. Let your imagination go; there are no restrictions here. Spend some time at this exercise.

Your list might look something like this:

WHAT I'D LIKE TO DO DURING MY LIFETIME
- Sail to Hawaii
- Write a novel
- Win a marathon (or at least complete one)
- Get a better paying job
- Get my college degree

Now look at the list you've made. What is your number one, above-all-else-I-must-do-this-before-I-die goal? It can be anything—to be the CEO of your company, to climb Mount Kilimanjaro, to write the all-time best-selling novel. Or it might be to take more training for your job, to learn to organize your time better, or to become a better manager of people. Whatever it is, it deserves a portion of your time.

I tackle the toughest jobs first. It gives me such a sense of accomplishment to cross them off my list, and I can then look forward to the rest of the day. —*Marie*

What happens to most of us is that this life goal, the thing that would bring meaning to our lives, gets put on a back burner while we pour ourselves into those urgent daily tasks and pressures that have little lasting significance in our lives. Because we never get to the thing that is most important to us, we feel frustrated and sometimes even angry. Stress is the end result.

It is essential that we take some time each day to work on our life goal. For me, writing is a life goal. It's my creative outlet, the artesian well that brings freshness to my life, the underground river of purpose for me. Since I work full-time as a managing editor, and since I am a morning person, most mornings I'm up writing long before dawn. I don't turn out a lot of pages each day, but if I write even one page and keep at it day after day, before long I have a book.

So mark your number one life goal *A-1*. You might even want to mark it with a colored highlighter.

Write a novel A-1

Now look at the other items you've written on your list. Which of them are the most important, can't-live-without-doing-this goals? Mark them in some way, such as with a letter *A*. Then you can go back and rank all the top priority items as A-1, A-2, etc., in the order of their importance.

Get a better paying job A-2
Get my college degree A-3

Look at the list again. Note all those things that should be done but are not as important as the first batch. Mark them with a *B*, and number them as well.

Sail to Hawaii B-1
Win a marathon B-2

Look at the list for a third time. Is there anything left that *absolutely* must be done? If the answer is no, then free yourself—dump the rest of the list. Life won't stop because you've dumped it. In fact, life just might start for you—because now your priorities are in order and you'll be spending your time doing those things that fulfill you.

A PLAN FOR SURVIVAL
Now that you know what's truly important to you, we're ready for a plan for survival, both at home and on the job.

First of all, acknowledge that you need a plan. You'll be surprised how little planning time is needed once you've determined what's important to you. About ten minutes at night or a few minutes in the morning, with a weekly checkup to see how you're doing, is all that's needed.

Here's how to do it: Each morning (or the night before), write down the day's top priorities. When you're doing this, don't forget that A-1 priority, your life goal, the thing you want to do before you die. Squeeze out a few minutes in the day for that priority. It will give you a sense of purpose, of working toward something truly important to you, and it will make everything else easier to face.

It might work best to write your priorities on a calendar. If you have a complex schedule, an hourly calendar helps to keep it all straight. But if the thought of ever getting *that* organized causes you to despair, just make a quick, simple list on a notepad, like this:

MAY 2

- Have devotions before the kids get up.
- Put in a load of wash before work.
- Pick up kids after school and drop them off at piano lessons.
- While they are taking lessons, shop for groceries.
- If there is time, have the car serviced.
- Take kids shopping for shoes.
- Light supper of soup and sandwiches [since you'll be late].
- Put kids to bed.
- Spend a few minutes doing research for my novel.

Throughout the day, enjoy the satisfaction of crossing items off your list. Done! Finished! Yeah!

For a number of years I've used a system that I find very simple and very effective.

I set up a three-by-five-inch card file with four sections. In each section the cards are a different color for easy identification. Section one has only one card in it, on which I've listed daily tasks. Section two has seven cards in it, on which I've listed one major task for each day of the week. Section three has thirty-one cards, one for each day of the month. Each card has a suggested ten-minute task. Sometimes I do these, sometimes I don't. But if I faithfully do the thirty-one tasks, a lot of little things get taken care of and never become big tasks. The fourth section has twelve cards, one for each month of the year. There are certain tasks that are seasonal, biannual (happening twice a year), or annual. No need to try to remember these—just list them on cards and pull out the appropriate month's card at the beginning of that month. Such a plan helps us to free our memories and minds for something more important. Here are some ideas to get you started.

DAILY TASKS AT HOME (MORNING)
- Fix breakfast and clean up.
- Make lunch(es) at the same time.
- Make bed(s) or oversee the making of beds.
- Pick up clothing, toys, newspapers, and magazines.
- Use a soiled towel to wipe down bathroom fixtures, then toss the towel in the washer.
- Run a load of wash (probably necessary if you have a family).

DAILY TASKS AT HOME (EVENING)
- Use commuting time to unwind if possible. Read something light and fun if you're on public transportation. Listen to favorite music tapes if you're driving. Talk to your kids if you pick them up from school.
- When you arrive home, give the kids a small snack—carrots or apple slices—and find a quiet corner for yourself for just a few minutes. I know

it's hard to find time for yourself, but it will make a difference if you can do it.

- Change clothes. By changing clothes you are mentally shifting roles from worker to homemaker.
- Enlist as much help as you can for the dinner hour. Husbands and teens can cook. School-age kids can make salads, cook certain things, set the table, and help with cleanup. This is a great time for kids to fill you in on their lives or have you help with homework.
- Exercise. A walk with a husband or a child is not only a good time for exercise, but a good time for communicating as well. Maybe your forte is aerobics, swimming, or bicycling. When possible include a family member, since together time is limited in families where Mom works.
- Plan what to wear tomorrow, including hose and accessories. (Have your kids get their clothes ready, too, or do it for them if they're too young.)
- Choose one task from your "weeklies" list of household chores and do that. Resist the temptation to do more.
- Spend a few minutes on your A-1 top priority goal for your life.

DAILY TASKS FOR THE OFFICE WORKER

- Organize for the day by checking calendar and/or tickler file. (A tickler file is a file folder for each day of the month and one for each month of the year. It's a great place to drop papers, notes, and other scheduling information. Just be sure to check the file each morning before starting the day's work.)

- If you have a secretary or assistant(s), spend a few minutes outlining the day's tasks and priorities.
- At the end of the day, spend a few minutes filing papers in a tickler file.
- See what was left undone today and add it to tomorrow's list.
- Straighten your desk so that in the morning it will look inviting rather than threatening.

DAILY TASKS FOR OTHER TYPES OF JOBS
- Find out what's expected of you for the day.
- Think through how you are going to accomplish those tasks.
- Allow time for paperwork or cleanup at the end of the day, if necessary.
- Determine what you need to do during your lunch break.

WEEKLY TASKS
Write one of these on each of seven cards, labeled for each day of the week (Monday, Tuesday, etc.). Each day, look at the appropriate card and try to do its task.

- Clean the refrigerator.
- Plan the week's menus.

Rising early helps me get some housework tasks out of the way before I do my jobs of preschool teaching and giving piano lessons. —**Bettina**

- Dust the furniture and vacuum the floors in two rooms.
- Clean the oven and burners of the stove.
- Change the beds, wash the sheets, and remake the beds (avoids a lot of folding).
- Do touch-up ironing (best to eliminate anything requiring much time to iron).
- Look for rips, tears, missing buttons, etc. Either fix them then or set them aside for another night.

MONTHLY TASKS

Write one of these on each of thirty-one cards, labeled 1–31. Each day, look at the card for that date and try to do its task.

- Clean one kitchen drawer.
- Sort through one closet.
- Write one friend a note.

Remember that the tasks on this list are the kind that can go undone without stopping the world. But if you can do them, you'll be surprised at how well you'll keep up with things. If you can't do one day's task, put the card to the back of the file. It will come up again next month.

YEARLY TASKS

Once a month check one of your twelve cards or your yearly list to see what's needed this month. Your cards might look like this:

JANUARY
- Buy Christmas gift wrap on sale.
- Buy bed linens on sale.
- Get the tax information gathered together.

FEBRUARY
- Clean the condenser coils on the refrigerator.
- Make an appointment with a tax accountant.

Learning to work with such a system is a matter of making your lists or cards and then remembering to refer to them. Checking them could be a part of your morning planning time.

RESOURCES AND TOOLS TO HELP
YOU PLAN YOUR TIME
Daily Planners
Visit a stationery or business-office supply store, and you will be overwhelmed by the variety of daily planning books that are available. A daily planner with a Christian emphasis, *Fruit of Her Hands,* is published by Focus on the Family. Because it is undated, it is possible to start using it at any time, even in the middle of the year.

Erasable/Write-on Calendars
Erasable calendars are also available from office supply stores. These are great for yearlong planning, either for your business or for your family. Some of the calendars have space for more than one year for truly long-term planning.

I constantly make lists. I had an assistant once who said I need a to-do list to go to the ladies' room! I am constantly juggling priorities between various work projects, and I find that daily and weekly to-do lists are the best way to stay on top of things. —*Jan*

MORE TIPS FOR SAVING TIME AT HOME

- Keep everything as simple as possible. Complicated systems, tools, appliances, clothing, and processes only take more time.
- Divide big jobs into many smaller ones. Alan Lakein, the founder of modern time management, calls this "Swiss cheesing." It means you poke holes in a big job by doing little pieces of it until finally it's completed.
- Stop trying to be perfect. Leave that to the "ladies of leisure."
- Get help from anyone who will help (more in the next chapter).
- Buy duplicates of items that are in high demand—combs, hair spray, toothpaste, shoelaces—to avoid emergency trips to the store.
- Make up and duplicate a standard permission form for your kids. Fill in date and activity, sign, and return to school.
- Have a special place for your keys, your purse, the kids' schoolbooks, and any other items that are continually being lost.
- Try to do two things at once—talk on the phone and clean cupboards, watch television and mend.

- When you have shopping and errands, make a night of it. Plan your route from one shopping place to the next so that there is no backtracking. Shop stores by going around in a loop.
- Buy postage stamps by mail or phone.
- Use delivery services as much as possible.

MORE TIPS FOR SAVING TIME AT THE OFFICE

- Make a decision about each piece of paper as you pick it up — deal with it, delay it (put it in the proper file), delegate it, or drop it (in the trash).
- Ask, "Is this meeting necessary?"
- Group your phone calls — do a bunch of them at the same time.
- Read smart, not fast. You don't have to read everything that crosses your desk.
- Tear out articles that you might want to read but don't have time to read now.
- Use your lunch hour or coffee breaks to place catalog orders by phone.

Watch popular women's magazines for more tips. Almost every issue carries at least one article related to saving time.

Does it all still seem overwhelming — too much for any one human being to do? It probably is. So let's see what can be done about that. In the next chapter we're going to look at ways to involve others in helping out.

SUGGESTED READING

Alan Lakein, *How to Get Control of Your Time and Your Life* (New York: NAL-Dutton, 1989). This book is a classic — the definitive book on gaining control of your time and life.

Michael LeBoeuf, *Working Smart: How to Accomplish More in Half the Time* (New York: Warner Books, 1988).

Karen S. Linamen and Linda Holland, *Working Women, Workable Lives: Creative Solutions for Managing Home and Career* (Wheaton, Ill.: Harold Shaw, 1993).

Alec Mackenzie, *Time Trap: The New Version of the 20-Year Classic on Time Management* (New York: AMACOM, 1991).

Sybil Stanton, *The Twenty-Five-Hour Woman: The Guilt-Free Way to Manage Your Time* (New York: Bantam, 1990).

Amy Vanderbilt, *Organize Your Life* (New York: Doubleday, 1966).

Gwen Weising, *Finding Time for Family Fun* (Grand Rapids: Baker, 1991).

CHAPTER 3

Getting Help

I recently saw a cartoon caption that read, "When I'm down in the dumps, I ask my relatives why they don't clean the place." It's a twisted kind of humor for working women, because it is too close to the truth.

An article by Charles Whited in the *Denver Post* stated:

> The fact is, a woman who does her job in this crazy society does several of them. And if she goes out to earn a living too, the so-called "woman's work"—the menial laundry, housecleaning, cooking, sewing, bed making and all the rest—don't just disappear; they're waiting when she gets home.[1]

We used to have a saying when I was growing up: "Who was your servant last year?" It was used when one person felt the other was asking too much of him—most often between siblings. The working woman of the household can often justifiably ask this question. A woman who takes on full-time employment, for whatever reason, simply must have help if she is even to survive, let alone thrive. She

I rent my extra bedrooms to a single mom and her son. We trade child care. She works nights and we watch her son. When I work evenings she's here with my teen. —*Sue*

cannot be everyone's servant—although that may have been the family's lifestyle in the past.

I was amazed in looking through the questionnaires from which the sidebars for this chapter were drawn. Many had left blank the question How do you get the help you need at home? It tells me that many women aren't getting help they need and don't know how to get it. One woman answered, "I yell and stomp my feet a lot." That was probably one of the most honest answers given!

In this chapter we'll look at the problem and make some suggestions about how and where to get help. We will offer ideas to help working women get to a place of thriving by making sure everyone is sharing the workload, both at work and at home.

WHO WAS YOUR SERVANT LAST YEAR?

Perhaps the "servant last year" was the wife/mother. If she was not a working woman then, the chances are that she did more for her family than was necessary for their survival. We women seem to do that. It's called spoiling. And if that has been the case in your home, a major retraining needs to happen when you take a job.

Then there are families who don't really understand what it costs the working woman in terms of health and strength to have a full-time job. Many women go to work full-time and never seem to miss a beat. A commercial of several years ago probably should have been banned from television for the misinformation it communicated. It was about a woman who could bring home the bacon, fry it up in the pan, and still be everything her man needed her to be.

That's a myth that is superdestructive to superwomen. The truth is, we *cannot* do it all. We cannot be all things to all people. There has to be a time for spiritual, physical, mental, and emotional renewal.

The price a woman and her family pay for her trying to do it all is just too great. Eventually she will burn out, and then the whole family will suffer. So it really doesn't matter who was your servant last year; *this year it has to be different.* Everyone in the family has to get involved in serving other members of the family. Come to think of it, Jesus kind of gave us that idea when he was on earth, didn't he?

JUST ASK

Everything I read points to one fact: Most of us fail to get the help we need because we don't ask — or don't know how to ask — for it. Whether we need help at home or in the workplace, the same holds true. A secretary won't know what you need unless you tell her. A coworker won't know you can't lift a heavy box unless you say so. Your husband will be clueless as to your plans for the house unless you tell him. It's amazing how our strengths and weaknesses transfer from office to home and back again.

So let's look at some principles for successful delegating in the business world. And as you're reading this, think about ways these principles might transfer to delegating at home.

1. Decide what you want done. Set goals, and make them measurable and specific.

Linda was a manager of a small staff. She was struggling with her personnel, often wondering, *Why don't they know what I want? Why can't they get inside my head?* Such thinking is counterproductive and leads to a great deal of frustration and lack of communication with the staff. There is no way another person can get inside your head. Goals must be set forth and clearly defined (in writing is best). It is not enough to say, "This year we want to increase productivity." Increase productivity? In what ways? By how much? Who's going to do it? How?

It would be so much better to say, "This year we want to increase productivity by 15 percent. That means that each of us must do one additional project over what we did last year. If we do, we should see an increase in revenue of fifty thousand dollars. Now, team, do you think we can do it? How do you see us accomplishing our goal?"

If you are not in management, then it is your responsibility to see that your leader defines goals specifically. Keep asking for definition until you are sure what is being asked of you. Take responsibility for yourself.

2. Be aware that if our needs change, we have to inform our staff.
There is no way staff members can know that what was top priority a week ago is no longer a priority. Staff is often not privy to information coming to a manager in decision-making meetings.

And if you are not in management, you need to be aware of changing needs. Sometimes busy management fails to inform you, and all of a sudden you realize there's been a shift of priorities. Ask. Find out why.

3. Pick the right person for the job.
Nothing is more frustrating or devastating to an employee than to be in the wrong job. But when you find the right person for the right job, then you can back off and let her do the job with little or no supervision. The individual's self-esteem goes sky-high, and you are freed to give your attention and energies to something else.

When you are evaluating candidates for a particular job, not only are their qualifications important, but so is their interest in the project. You may find someone who has a lot of interest in the project but little time to do it. That's the wrong candidate. If you find someone who has a lot of time but little interest, that also is the wrong person.

If you are not in a leadership position but see a project come along in which you have a great interest and that you also feel qualified to carry out, let your boss know. You may solve a big problem for your boss, simply because you've volunteered and he doesn't have to look for someone else. If you have a great interest in the project but feel underqualified, ask if you can have the project, and ask too for the training necessary to accomplish the task. And that brings us to our next point.

4. Train the person for the job.
One of the great deficiencies in business today is the lack of training for a particular job. It is unfair to expect anyone to do a job he is unprepared to do. That is a setup for failure; it is frustrating to management and devastating to the inexperienced worker.

Training may seem time consuming and expensive, but in the long run it is not. It is the only way to get the best out of staff members, to preserve their self-esteem, and to obtain the kind of results we want. As a manager, I am forever looking for opportunities for staff training. One of my biggest frustrations in the past has been to work for a company that ignores or devalues training.

If you are a nonmanagement worker in such a situation, request training. If formal training is not forthcoming, ask for subscriptions to newsletters and magazines that relate to your work.

Then there is a point at which you say, "This is my life and my future. If this company is not going to pay to see me trained, I'll take care of it myself. It is an investment in myself."

Deb is a single mom who has worked very hard to keep a roof over the heads of herself and her child and wheels under both of them. She has no support from her ex-husband.

Just recently she signed up for extension courses with a well-known university, and she is studying about leadership, which includes leadership in the workplace. There is some expense involved; there are books to purchase, etc. There is also an investment of time. But this is a lady who is not going to wait for someone to hand her this kind of specialized training. She is taking the matter into her own hands. She is making an investment in herself.

5. *Check on the worker without hovering.*

We need to make certain the worker fully understands the goals in mind for a project, which includes its importance to the company and the process to achieve the goal. And we should set up specific checkpoints at which we will review the progress and be available to answer any questions. Then we need to back off and let him have the fun of figuring out how to make it work.

If this is a new worker, or if it is the first time through the process, there will need to be more checkpoints than if the worker is experienced. It is worth the investment of time to see that the worker succeeds, and succeeds well, on a first-time project. Self-esteem goes up, quality of work goes up, and next time you will be working with a well-trained worker.

But note that there is a fine line between checking on a worker and hovering. No one likes to be given a job without being trusted with the responsibility. So while you need checkpoints, try to avoid repeatedly asking things like "How's it going?" or "Let me see what you've done so far." Those kinds of statements communicate to the worker that you really don't trust him. Don't hover.

6. Be available for further training.
It is extremely frustrating to need specific guidance and training and not have it as a project progresses. If you are in a supervisory position, you need to be accessible to employees for input, guidance, information, and direction for the project. Empower people to do the job you've asked them to do by giving them the necessary resources.

7. Give them the whole task.
If possible—if the worker is ready— hand over the entire task and step

*A*sk! Sometimes I think my husband and kids can read my mind. They can't. When I ask, they help. —*Monica*

away from it. It's freeing and professionally satisfying to both of you.

It's important to remember that some projects are too big for one person. In that case it's essential to either let the project manager get the help needed or assign others to the task yourself.

If you are a worker, you should expect the procedure listed above from your leadership. If it is not forthcoming, sit down with your employer and discuss it.

8. Try not to give the same "awful" job to the same person time after time.

After someone learns a job, especially a difficult or unpleasant one, it's easy to keep handing that job off to the same person. He or she is trained, efficient, and maybe even willing, but it's not fair, and in time the worker will rebel, give up, or become less efficient.

If you are a worker and you feel all the undesirable jobs are being dumped on you, it's time to speak up: Talk to your employer, ask for a different assignment. Make sure your supervisor knows the problem is this particular job and not work in general. Avoid giving the impression that you are lazy.

9. Keep cool when someone makes a mistake.

Mistakes will happen. In fact, in some well-known companies there is concern if no mistakes are made. It means there are no risks being taken, no new learning taking place, and no new ideas being implemented. A mistake is just that—a mistake. Hopefully it won't be an expensive mistake, but sometimes even expensive mistakes can be a great learning tool.

So keep your cool when an employee blows it. If you overreact, you will soon be managing by fear, and that is one of the most unhealthy workplace environments of all. Fearful employees are always looking over their shoulder to see who's coming after them. They spend an inordinate amount of time writing memos and leaving a paper trail to make sure their tails are covered. When you're looking back, there is no way to look toward the future.

As a worker in such an environment, you have to weigh the value of the position against the cost to you in terms of mental and emotional health. You have to ask, Is this job worth it, or could I be doing something that would be better for me and less stressful? Do I want to spend the rest of my working career looking over my shoulder?

APPLY DELEGATING PRINCIPLES TO THE PEOPLE YOU LIVE WITH

The principles given above are tested and tried in the marketplace, and we know they work there. But you may not realize the same principles work in the home as well. If we're smart, we can integrate what we're learning on the job into the whole of our lives.

Let's see how this might work.

1. Decide what you want done. Set goals, and make them measurable and specific.

A lot of the reason we don't get help at home is because the people we live with don't know what we want done. For their sanity and ours, we need to decide. Our goals have to be reasonable and measurable. If our family members are given goals that are too tough for them, or if they are not sure what they are supposed to do, we set them up for failure, and we set ourselves up for frustration—lots of it.

I told my husband that at home I felt like I was the manager and he was the assistant. What I needed was for him to be my comanager. By putting my emotions into concrete terms that he could relate to, I was able to help him understand. —*June*

What are some measurable goals that could be posted someplace where every family member could see them? (Get the family to help formulate the goals. People buy into goals better if they've had a part in shaping them.) Here's one example:

Our goal is to have the house livable by the time we all leave for work and school in the morning.

That means:

- Your bed made
- Your breakfast dishes in dishwasher
- Your wet towels in the washer
- Your dirty clothes in the hamper
- Your animals fed and put in their place for the day [If there is only one family pet, this chore must be assigned to a different person each day or week.]

Could anyone misunderstand the goal? To make it more fun and not so threatening, post an estimated time for each task. That way your helpers at home can try to "beat the clock." They can also see that this job isn't so bad, since Mom thinks it will take only five minutes to complete. Or perhaps you could use a chart as a reminder

48

and let everyone check off by his name what he did that morning.

2. Be aware that if our needs change, we have to inform family members.

Most husbands and children are notoriously poor at mind reading. Because we women are intuitive by nature, we often think their lack of ability to know what we are thinking without being told is a plot to frustrate us. In most cases, it isn't. They honestly do not know that our needs or the needs of the family have changed. It is our responsibility to tell them.

Listing new tasks on a chores chart is one way to let them know that it's now summer instead of winter, so we need the sprinklers moved rather than the snow shoveled. (I'm being facetious, but sometimes it's almost that bad!)

Sit down with your helpers and tell them what's currently a priority and why. This kind of a discussion can be a marvelous experience for children in learning how to manage their own time and life.

3. Pick the right person for the job.

You know almost innately how to do that at work, but at home you may miss it. In order for the home helper to be successful, tasks need to be tailored to his size, motor skills, maturity, and ability. If you want to frustrate a child until he gives up, then constantly give him a task that is too difficult for him. Constant failure — never being able to measure up to expectations — is demoralizing to anyone. It will damage and perhaps destroy a child's self-esteem.

On the other hand, when the job is tailored to his abilities, he's able to make a contribution to the family and to please someone he cares about—his mom. This can be extremely affirming for a child.

In my management positions I have always tried to stretch my employees in their skills. I try to hand them something just a little too hard so that they are challenged, but not so hard that I set them up for failure. It works for employees, and it works for children as well.

It's also a good idea to consider how much interest your child has in a particular job. Some kids love to cook, some don't mind doing the wash. I know I'm an odd duck, but when I was growing up I used to love to do the ironing for Mom. My dad was a big man who wore chambray work shirts, and ironing them was a lot like ironing a big blue tent. I also had two brothers who wore cotton shirts, and I often ironed about twenty or thirty shirts at a time.

I felt good about the contribution I was making to the entire family. I was glad I could do something that *really* helped my mom.

4. Train the person for the job.

This is frequently the point at which failure takes place, both in the workplace and in the home.

Most kids love to help. They just need to know how to do the job in a way that pleases you. Investing some time in teaching children the way you want things done will reap a huge reward in help. Here are some ideas for teaching a child a job:

- Go slowly. Just how slowly is determined by the age and development of the child.
- Don't give too many instructions at once.

Although the child may be in a hurry to see the whole picture, take it slowly.

- Make sure the child understands what you want. Have him repeat your instructions back to you.
- Offer lots of praise as he accomplishes each step.
- Review at every stage until you are sure he understands.
- Finally, let him try the whole process on his own. Be aware he will make mistakes the first few times. Allow for that. Encourage him, praise him, and give him a chance to try again.

Before you know it, you have a child who makes a bed without lumps, who can set the table and put the silverware in the right place, who can make a salad and not have it all over the kitchen. This child has become a wonderful helper to you.

A word about husbands. They should have been taught how to do certain household tasks, but many have missed this step in their education. When they were growing up, they were not given the opportunity to learn how to help. They too may need clear explanations of what kind of help you need.

Some men have learned to help, but they do things the way their mother did them or make up their own way. If it is not the way you want it done, then you owe it to your husband and to your relationship to explain your way of doing the task. And you may have to explain or remind him several times until it sinks in. Most husbands want to please their wives, and it is our responsibility to show them what will please us. (Also, be open to the possibility that your

husband's way may be better than the way you do something. If so, learn and be grateful.)

5. Check on the worker without hovering.
After you're sure you can turn the task over to a family
member, leave him alone. Let him do it. Allow for the fact
that he will find ways to adapt the task to his own work
style. Once in a while, check to see what's being done and
give just a little guidance if need be — not criticism, but
guidance. Exhibit the same courtesies and sensitivity you
would to a paid employee. Be gracious.

6. Be available for further training.
Just be there if the task starts to go awry. Help the helper
become successful.

7. Give them the whole task.
Have you ever heard, "Hey, I thought that was my job.
How come Cindy's doing it?" or "I wanted to help you,
Mom, and now you're doing it. How come?" How come,
indeed. Give your helpers the job and keep out of it.

Here's an area Linda didn't do well in. She gave responsibilities to her husband and children but then took them
back. After two or three times, they gave up and let her do
it. Since she was a full-time working woman, it wasn't long
until she collapsed under the strain of it all. One day she
looked up and wondered what had happened.

Give them the task and let them do it — their way!

*8. Try not to give the same "awful" job to the same person time
after time.*
I think this may be a key factor in getting the help you need.
Who wants to be the one to always carry out the garbage

or clean the toilets? These are not fun jobs. But there are some jobs that are fun.

The other night I was selecting oranges at the produce counter of a grocery store. A young boy was also selecting oranges. I watched him for a moment because of his concentration and because of the obvious care with which he was making his choices. After he had bagged a dozen or so, he hoisted them onto the scale and weighed them. About that time his mother appeared and said, "How are you doing?"

The whole thing made me feel good. Here was a young man who was genuinely helping his mother. It was obvious he felt good about the contribution he was making, and they were going to get out of the grocery store more quickly because he had been trained to help.

So give the helpers in your home variety in their tasks. Let them learn to cook (fun), shop for food (fun), clean the garage (not fun), sort and wash clothes (not the worst of tasks), clean the refrigerator (not fun), plant a garden (fun). And find out which tasks your kids think are fun or not fun, too—their preferences may be different from yours!

9. Keep cool when someone makes a mistake.
Why do we practice this at the office and not at home? I can assure you that if you are teaching your children or husband new ways to do things, they will make mistakes. Mistakes are part of the learning process. There is not much that is more destructive to a person's self-esteem than giving him a

I **express how I feel—stressed, like I can't get done all I need to do. Then I ask for the help I need.** *—Esther*

new task and expecting instant mastery.

What could possibly be gained by yelling at a child or spouse when something is not done the way you wanted it to be done? All you do is take the heart right out of them. There is no desire to try again. To do so would be something like volunteering for surgery without anesthesia.

To sum it all up, to get the help you need, delegate, delegate. Give the responsibility and the authority to others, whether at the office or in your home, and step back. Give the worker a chance to learn, ask questions, and try out his own approach to the task. Your job is to clearly define the task, encourage, be available to give more information, and trust the worker to carry out the job.

BUYING HELP

Another way to get the help you need is to buy it. Sometimes, for a working woman with an income, the best solution to keeping on top of housework is to spend part of her earnings on housecleaning, laundry, child care, or yard work. Sometimes the expense is an investment in the well-being of the family.

I remember the first time I hired a housekeeper. I felt so guilty that I couldn't do it all myself. After all, my mother had always managed both a job and our home. The guilt lasted about ten minutes—after that I enjoyed coming home on Friday night to a clean house. I enjoyed being able to take off on Saturday and have some time for recreation.

Only you can decide if you should pay for help. I think for many of us there's a small nagging thought that says, *The people I live with should be helping me. I shouldn't have to hire someone. I must be failing in my ability to enlist them—or to train them.* Our thinking might go so far as to say, *If they really loved me, they would help me.*

If that is in your thinking, it probably has nothing to do with the work. There is probably another underlying cause. Perhaps you have a martyr's complex. If so, it needs to be dealt with. It is so hard to live with a martyr.

Perhaps you're suffering from low self-esteem and you think—way down deep—that you can only prove your value if you can do everything and do it perfectly. You're trying to measure up to some other person's standard. It isn't worth it.

A number of years ago someone asked me, "Gwen, what drives you?" It was the beginning of a search to find out what did drive me. I found after a lot of counseling, prayer, and self-searching that I was performance oriented. I wanted everything to be perfect because I was suffering from low self-esteem. Of course, I could never reach the level of perfection I wanted, so I tried harder and worked more. And then I tried harder yet and worked even more.

Finally I identified the source of the problem and what was causing my low self-esteem. I took action to remedy the problem, and I am now in what some call recovery, which simply means you are aware of what's wrong and you have to watch yourself all the time so as not to fall back into the same patterns and traps again.

I still work hard, but it comes from a different place in me. Now I want to do a good job for others. Now I want to bless others with my work. Now I do many things for me because I enjoy doing them. It has nothing to do with proving who I am. It feels good. (We'll be talking more about work addiction and its causes in a later chapter.)

I **have a maid who comes once a week, and my daughter has assigned chores.**

—*Diane*

So buy the help you need. You don't have to do it all to prove who you are and that you have value. And in the area of paying for the help you need, I don't think there's anything wrong with paying your children to do the work you'd pay someone else to do.

Deb was paying a cleaning lady until her nine-year-old daughter said, "I can do what she's been doing." So they tried it out, and sure enough, she could do it. Deb is watching so that if Jamie gets tired of doing the cleaning, she can be relieved of the task. She doesn't want a nine-year-old cleaning-burnout victim on her hands.

I used to pay my son to vacuum for me. He enjoyed it (or at least the money), it was a great help to me, and it kept the money in the family.

What tasks are you doing or paying someone else to do that you could pay your own child to do?

GETTING HELP BY BARTERING

There's another way to get the help you need, and that is by bartering your goods or services. Bartering is as old as time and was the means of exchange long before there was money. We often think of bartering as a way to get goods or commodities without spending money. But it can also be used to get *help* without spending money. Anyone can pay someone else to help them if there is enough money available. But if you don't have money, then you can barter for time and help.

There are some tasks that require a large block of time — a larger block of time than a working woman has if she's going to take care of her family's physical needs. So don't take care of their needs. Wait a minute before you start throwing rocks. Just for a day, let someone else take care of the kids while you paper the bathroom, paint the kitchen, or wax the hardwood floors. But remember, this is a barter. What do you have to exchange? Could you watch the other person's children while she has her day to catch up on tasks? Do you have a gift for cooking or sewing that you could offer in exchange for her time?

So how do we get started in bartering? First, make a list of what you need that you don't have. It might not be time. It might be a tool, clothes, or experience. Then make a list of what you have to offer. At first you might think you have little to offer, but keep thinking. We just get so used to our own gifts that we don't think they are unusual or have much value. But they are valuable to someone who needs something done and doesn't have your gift. Or maybe you have something tangible to offer, like the use of your lawn mower or your camping equipment.[2]

Post your list in local grocery stores, on church bulletin boards, and at work. Say something like "Will exchange the use of my camping equipment for help in cleaning my garage. Must be able to haul away trash."

You can even barter with your kids and spouse. "I'll take your clothes to the cleaners on my way to work if you'll write the checks for the bills." Remember, bartering is a skill that is acquired with practice. Keep thinking about it, and ask God for creativity in this area.

RESOURCES FOR GETTING THE HELP YOU NEED

The Servicemaster Corporation has been a leader in innovation for many years. They seem to be sensitive to the culture and to the needs of working women. One of their companies is Merry Maids, a franchised housecleaning service set up to follow strict guidelines. The services of the company can be used periodically to help you catch up or on a weekly basis.

They also have developed a company called Helpmaster. This is a personal service that assists busy people. They will do your grocery shopping, take your mother to the doctor, or do most anything you need done.

You can also look in the pages of your local telephone directory under Housecleaning for reputable firms to help you.

SUGGESTED READING

Mindy Bingham and Sandy Stryker, *More Choices: A Strategic Planning Guide for Mixing Career and Family* (Santa Barbara, Calif.: Advocacy, 1987).

Faye J. Crosby, *Juggling: The Unexpected Advantages of Balancing Career and Home for Women and Their Families* (New York: Free Press, 1993).

Ronnie Eisenberg and Kate Kelly, *Organize Your Family: Simple Routines for You and Your Kids* (New York: Hyperion, 1993).

Kathleen Koszyk, *Who Says You Can't Find Good Help Anymore? A Guide to Finding, Managing, and Keeping Good Domestic Help* (New York: Vantage, 1986).

Karen S. Linamen and Linda Holland, *Working Women, Workable*

Lives: Creative Solutions for Managing Home and Career (Wheaton, Ill.: Harold Shaw, 1993).

Linda F. Radke, *Nannies, Maids, and More: The Complete Guide for Hiring Household Help* (Scottsdale, Ariz.: Five Star, 1989).

Gwen Weising, *Finding Time for Family Fun* (Grand Rapids: Baker, 1991).

PART
TWO

*Thriving
on the Home Front*

CHAPTER 4

The Married Working Woman

From 1989 through the year 2000, 66 percent of new entrants to the labor force will be women. By 2000, 80 percent of women aged 25–54 will be working." So says a publication called *Marketing to Women*.[1] If this is true, then it is safe to assume that a good portion of those women are married, and that creates a whole world of interesting challenges, problems, and frustrations.

WHY IN THE WORLD WOULD A MARRIED WOMAN WORK?

Why, indeed? There are many reasons why married women work, and most of them are not too different from the reasons unmarried women work. But let's talk about some of them.

There are women who feel they have a calling in life. Some have trained to be doctors, lawyers, teachers, and a host of other serving professionals. These women feel that it is their reasonable service to do these jobs. It is their way of making a contribution to the well-being of mankind.

There are other women who work to give their families enough income to survive. When the job a husband has

If things are getting really crazy, I schedule time on the calendar for my family just like I do for other appointments.

—Marie

does not pay enough to maintain a quality lifestyle, an extra income can help. When a husband is attending school to pursue a dream or to better himself and must cut back on working hours to study, an extra income can be a financial lifesaver. When a husband loses his job for whatever reason—downsizing of his company, choosing not to relocate, resigning because of frustration on the job, or just plain being fired—there may be no alternative but for the wife to take a job.

Then there are the benefits of more income. It's almost impossible for young couples to purchase a home of their own on one income. The cost of housing has skyrocketed steadily over the last few years. And there's the cost of private schools for the children. Many Christian parents feel there is no alternative but to put their children in private schools, due to the current state of public education in this country.

Some couples want to offer their children the benefits of travel, college, or living in a better neighborhood. All of these are made more accessible by the addition of another income.

There are some women who just like to work outside the home. They like the challenge, the mental stimulation, and the interaction with others they find in the marketplace. They like to see what they can accomplish.

I have an amazing friend named Sue, who got tired of the

corporate life and started her own company. It's a product development company. She names some of the biggest publishers and catalogers in the country among her clients.

Sue is extremely successful—so successful that she has to spend a good deal of time traveling, servicing her many accounts. I think Sue works because she's good at what she does, she's always worked, and she likes what she does. I don't think she has to work for financial reasons; she's married to a dentist with a very successful practice. These two have a charming relationship of friendship and trust. It's a beautiful thing to see. But the point is, Sue is one of those women who simply enjoys working outside the home.

So women work for many reasons, not all of which are associated with dollars. Of course, as in most areas of our lives, there is a trade-off. Being a working woman has many benefits, but it also has its down side. And learning to thrive in spite of the difficulties is what this book is all about.

WHAT IS THE SECRET TO MAKING A TWO-CAREER MARRIAGE WORK?

In a recent *Los Angeles Times* poll conducted in two southern California counties, working parents, particularly men, believed strongly that the demands of the wife's job were taking their toll at home. And while it was recognized that two incomes were a necessity, these people felt their parenting suffered as a result.[2]

Not only does the job of parenting suffer because both parents work; so can a marriage suffer because there is little time for the husband and wife to devote to one another. The problem is increased if they have children at home. So, can a two-career marriage work, and if it can, how? I read an interesting and wonderful article in *Reader's Digest* once that discussed common factors of happy marriages.[3] Let's look at some of them.

Happy couples feel at home with each other.
They are friends. They like to spend time with each other. It will probably help a two-career couple if they like to be together. They will probably make being together a priority and will be careful to make the time to do it.

Happy couples share routines and dreams.
This seems to be a vitally important concept. Many working women I've talked to recently are looking for a partnership in marriage. This includes laying down traditional roles and working together to make the whole relationship successful. Does it really matter who takes out the garbage, diapers a baby, makes dinner, or gets the car serviced? Perhaps tasks should be divided along the lines of abilities and not of traditional gender roles.

The important thing is that couples share dreams and goals and work together to make something bigger than both of them. Often couples start out with little or nothing in terms of possessions, and for many, the happiest times are those years of struggling to see a dream come true. Couples who have no goals toward which they can work, who have no common purpose to fulfill, often see their marriage run into big trouble. There has to be something bigger than both of you toward which you work.

Raising children is an all-consuming job, and if you do it right, it is a task that will occupy a good portion of your time, energy, resources, and strength. Raising children is a common purpose that parents must work together to accomplish. But beware when that goal is fulfilled. Counselors' offices across the country are filled with couples whose goal of raising their kids has been achieved, and all of a sudden, they have no other goal toward which they can work as a couple.

Happy couples learn to change.
Once upon a time the husband may have gotten up and gone to work each morning while the wife stayed home to sweep and bake bread. But now, perhaps, they both go to a job, and that changes everything. It is essential that the two people in a marriage be willing to change, to be flexible, to learn to help each other—and to drop the unessential in order to provide quality time for each other.

A wife who goes to work cannot simply add a job to everything else she does and still hope to have strength left for a quality relationship. A husband who has a working wife must understand this and must get involved in helping out. If he does not see the whole picture, his wife must talk with him and devise a plan that works for both of them.

My son's friend was talking with him about husbands of working women. She said that men often do a chore around the house and then that's it. They don't realize it has to be done day in and day out, not just once a week or once a month.

The *L.A. Times* article concluded, "'There's a lot of pressure now for men to say they would like to spend more time with their families,' but little evidence showing they do, said Mary Mattis, vice president of research for Catalyst. 'For the most part, women are still working two jobs.'"[4] An article in *Working Woman* magazine stated that in industrialized countries, men work an average of fifty hours a week at a job and around the house. The working wife works an average of eighty hours.[5]

I don't blame men entirely. Too many women don't say anything. They don't express their needs. Some feel a fair amount of guilt over the fact that they are working. Therefore, they try to cover that guilt by not making waves for anyone else in the family, particularly their husband. They want to avoid hearing, "It's been this way ever since you went to work" or "If you weren't working, this would have been taken care of."

It is essential that a couple sit down together and talk through the implications of a wife's working. And that is best done before she starts looking for a job. This would also be a good time to discuss why she is going to work. What are the goals? Talk, too, about what will happen with the money. Who will handle it? Realize you are probably raising your financial lifestyle, and if she ever wants to quit, it will make a drastic difference.

All of this to say that if a wife goes to work and if the couple wants to be happy about it, they'll both have to make some changes.

Happy couples understand the importance of sex.
You can talk all you want about sex and say that it is not what good marriages are about. But "scratch the surface calm of these marriages and frequently a strong and vibrant sexuality, a clear sexual chemistry, soon reveals itself." So says author Catherine Johnson.[6]

Good sex takes time. It has been said that sex starts in the head, not in bed. It is the culmination of friendship, companionship, and passion between two people. There is no way you can rush companionship. It absolutely requires talking, being together, sharing new ideas and insights, laughing and playing together. It requires a commitment of time.

That kind of sexual relationship is rich and fulfilling for both people involved. It avoids one or the other feeling used. It prevents someone from feeling he or she is just another item on an agenda—that one must get sex finished to get on to the next activity on the list. It quickly becomes a matter of priorities. Just what or who is most important in your life? Is that person worth your time?

Happy couples do not struggle for the upper hand.
Why do most of us persist in trying to control each other? It's all right to fight. In fact, it's healthy to fight, and it's important to learn how to fight fairly. Where two people live together, there will be conflict (or there should be if the relationship is healthy). But with happy couples the conflict is not about control, power, and status. It is about finding solutions to problems.

These people do not have an attitude that says, "That's woman's work"; nor an attitude that says, "I'm too good to do this." There is also no room in these marriages for an I'm-in-charge-and-that-means-I'm-in-charge-of-the-money-too mentality.

Happy couples usually describe their mate as their best friend.
And best friends love to be together. Best friends are sure life is going to

> hire a friend to clean my house twice a month. I declare Sunday a fun day—no chores, only family-outing and together time.
>
> —*Deborah*

end long before they've spent enough time together. If you like your husband, why wouldn't you want to spend time with him?

Suppose you are too busy to play together — games, hobbies, sports, vacations. Could you, perhaps, work together? Could you wax the car together and talk while you did so? Could you build a new room in the basement and pound nails together? Could you make the preparation of taxes a joint venture? Life isn't just about fun and vacations — it's about work, training children, maintenance of home, child care, elder care. Can you share all of life?

MY HUSBAND IS SO UNDERSTANDING

Is he? If he is, be thankful. Many husbands are glad to have their wives working and helping to provide some of the extras. Some are proud of their wives' accomplishments.

My son, in his twenties, is very proud of his mother and her working successes. He said once, "When I see you sitting there at your desk, wearing your glasses, I'm so proud of you." (I have been a managing editor since he was in junior high school.) Although at this time he is unmarried, he tells me he hopes his wife will work. He says he thinks it will give them more in common and they will have more to talk about. We then had a discussion about how he would have to help out at home if he expected his wife to carry part of the load of earning a living. He's part of a modern generation of men who are not threatened by a wife's ability to provide in part or in full.

I work with a young woman named Sydna. Long before this book is finished, she will have delivered her third child. I suppose she will take some time off before and after the baby is born. Sydna is the sole wage earner of their family. Her husband stays home with their children. He is not threatened by the arrangement. They have a loving and caring relationship, and they know they are each contributing an important part to the marriage and to the family.

There are some things we, as working women, can do to show consideration for a husband—whether he is supportive or not.

Never use the fact that you are working to help support the family as a weapon against him.

Some men still struggle with their inability to make enough to care for their families without their wives working. It is a threat to their ego. If you want to seriously damage your relationship, adopt a martyr spirit that lets him know you're only working because he's inadequate as a provider.

Never demand his help.

It's all right to expect it, to ask for it, but it will undo what you want to happen if you whine, pout, cry, or throw a fit because you don't think he's measuring up. A really good thing to do is to lower your expectations. Then everything that happens is positive. If you get a little help, it's great. If you get a lot of help, it's wonderful.

Don't come through the door at night griping and complaining about your job.

If you want to start a fight, this is a good way. Remember, after work you are both tired and hungry. You may also be coping with kids who are tired and hungry. If possible, take

We always eat dinner together no matter what the time. My daughter and I run together, and sometimes my husband joins us.

—Dianne

a few minutes to hide away and unwind, even before you talk to each other. Do what the British do, because it's a great idea: "Let's have a cup of tea, and then we can talk about it."

Don't tell your husband that your taking a job will not make any difference.

Yes, it will. It will make a huge difference. It's going to change the way all of you live forever. If you tell him it won't change anything, and then it does, he will be resentful. Once again, this is a decision the whole family must make. Some of the people you live with are going to have to look for their own socks.

Make time for him. Save a piece of time for him each day.

Maybe it's to sit with him in the bathroom while he shaves. Maybe it's those quiet moments after the last child has gone to bed.

If child care or schedules prevent the two of you from spending much time together in the evenings or mornings, why don't you consider lunch dates? Though brief, these can be wonderful times to renew your friendship. You might find yourself saving bits of information to share with each other at this time, especially if you have these lunch dates on a regular basis.

It's also important that the two of you get away together once in a while. It probably won't save a marriage if that marriage is already in trouble, but it won't hurt it either.

You need to talk with each other away from the daily responsibilities of life and without the interruption of your progenies' voices.

Win his support by asking lots of "What do you think?" kinds of questions.
And try to limit your "You should" statements. "What do you think about having a garden this year? Is that something you'd like to do?" This is opposed to "You told me you'd plant a garden this year. You should get started on it. Here it is the middle of April, and you haven't even raked up the leaves from last fall."

See the difference? You don't like shoulds, and neither does he. Shoulds and guilt are all tied up together. Many working women nearly "should" themselves to death because they feel guilty about working when they have a family. And many of us are very good about laying shoulds on the shoulders of not only husbands but all members of our family. Resist the temptation. It's not healthy for anyone, including you.

Resist the temptation to prove to others that your marriage is a good one.
If it is, be thankful and do whatever you and your husband need to do to keep it that way. It's really no one else's business how you arrange your life together. You don't have to prove that he doesn't resent or feel neglected by your working. To pursue any of this is a waste of time and emotional energy.

If there are people in your life who try to make you feel guilty about working—a mother, a mother-in-law, or some other person—ignore them. As long as the two of you are OK with your life, it's really nobody else's business.

Show an interest in his work.
Let him talk about his work with you. Be interested. Ask him to explain the parts you don't understand. Go with him to professional events, and learn to enjoy the people he works with.

I once knew a woman who refused to participate in her husband's world, although he begged her to accompany him. She was not interested in his professional life; she saw it as a threat and considered the people he worked with to be very unspiritual. I tried to encourage her to put on her best duds and go with him, but she would not. This was a symptom of a deeper problem, and she eventually lost her marriage.

You'll want to share with your husband about your job, too. You may even learn from him principles and ideas that could be applied to your work.

Resist the temptation to tell your husband and his associates how to run their business.
I can only imagine the disdain and disregard his associates would have for a meddling wife.

Honor your husband, his abilities, and his work in front of your children.
They will follow your example. It is to be hoped that he will honor you, your work, and your abilities before them also, so that they will honor you. This is grace-based living in an almost graceless world, and it is very appealing. It pleases God when each supports, loves, and cares for the other. It pleases God when you give priority to your marriage in

terms of time, energy, and consideration. He will bless you as a couple and as a family.

SOME JOBS ARE NOT COUPLE FRIENDLY

All right, so you love your job. It makes you feel good about yourself, important, maybe even powerful. Maybe the pay is wonderful. But it means that you're traveling a lot or working odd hours or working overtime or in some other way being taken away from those you love.

Something tells you your priorities are out of order. Something tells you that you need to make some changes, but it's so hard. You really want the job.

For many years it was men who were away from home working all kinds of impossible jobs, depriving their families of their presence. Today, in many cases, it's women who are away on business. A recent report says that women now constitute 40 percent of all workers in executive, administrative, and managerial occupations.[7] That's almost half of the managerial positions in this country. Management positions often require travel, dinner meetings, and other responsibilities that complicate a husband/wife relationship. I meet these women with their briefcases and overnight bags in airports all over the country.

If this scenario is yours, and if you value your marriage, maybe it's time to see what can be done to make your job marriage-friendly.

One possibility is that your *spouse* can make a job change that might make your two jobs work together better. Not all of the giving or giving up has to be on one side.

Though you have to find time for each other, it doesn't necessarily mean you have to give up your job, although you might. It could mean working at home part-time. It could mean flextime — becoming more available when your spouse is free. It could mean doing the same kind of job but closer to home, so less time is spent commuting. Or it could mean moving closer to your job.

But the cold, hard fact is that you might have to drop out of the employment scene for a time until life is less complicated. That would be a tremendous sacrifice and one that would require much prayer, but there are people who are making this decision.

Dr. Rebecca Wexler had just begun a residency program in radiology when her second child was born. She quit her job, knowing she might not be able to get back into the program later or at least that she wouldn't get back in at the same level. She is still committed to her career and reads radiology journals when the children are sleeping. She is not sorry for the decision she made.[8] If you are living a frantic life with no time for your husband and children, it's time to do something about it. I have a suspicion that once it's done, you'll be like Rebecca and not regret the decision.

IDEAS FOR GETAWAYS FOR THE TWO OF YOU

I knew a couple who got on a plane in Los Angeles to fly out to Catalina Island. But what the wife didn't know was that Catalina was just a stop along the way to a two-week vacation in Hawaii. Her husband had made all the arrangements, including the care of their preteen daughter. I thought that was one of the most charming things I had ever heard.

And then there was the woman who would occasionally leave home and check into a downtown hotel. She'd leave a note behind saying, "I'm at the _____ Hotel. I'll be dining at 7:30 P.M. and would love to see you then." Her husband would join her for a dinner rendezvous and a night away from home—and some much-needed time together.

But it doesn't need to be that elaborate. Getaway ideas can be as simple as a rendezvous in the park. You'll have to tailor your getaway plans to your circumstances: child-care needs, money, time, etc. Arrange for the kids to go to Grandma's or a friend's house for the evening, make a favorite dinner (or order in if you don't have time to cook), light the fireplace and the candles, put on some nice music, wear something beautiful, and prepare to enjoy the man you married.

Be creative; work at this business of togetherness. If you value your marriage, and I know you do, it's the most important thing you can do—far more important than your job. It really doesn't matter what you do as long as you do it together and enjoy the pleasure of each other's company. Here are some more ideas to get you thinking:

- Buy a new book and spend the evening reading it aloud to each other.
- Go for a walk or a hike together.
- Try a new sport together—golfing, sailing, ice-skating, or Rollerblading. (No, you're

When my children were still at home, we always went to dinner together on Friday evenings. Then we would rent a video to watch after dinner.

—Cathy

77

not too old! Why should kids have all the fun?)
- Save for a really wonderful vacation in some exotic place.
- Take in a sporting event that neither of you have seen before—ice hockey, wrestling, figure skating, water polo.
- Go to a cultural event such as an art exhibit, a ballet, a play.
- Plan and plant a garden together.
- Collect something together.
- Get a camera and see how many white churches, old school buildings, or other distinctive things you can photograph together.
- Bird-watch.

Find a good travel agent and be loyal to him or her. A travel agent will let you know when great travel opportunities present themselves. I have such an agent; while he tempts me with far more vacation opportunities than I can afford to take advantage of, I know once in a while he's going to hit it at the right time and I'm going to be able to do something I've only dreamed about.

Write the bureaus of tourism in places you'd like to visit. You'll soon have more information than you know what to do with. The information includes something in every price range.

Suggested Reading

Charlene Canape, *The Part-Time Solution: The New Strategy for Managing Your Career While Managing Motherhood* (New York: Harper and Row, 1990).

Betty Cittadine, *I Wish I Had a Wife: Sanity-Saving Tips for Working Moms* (Chicago: Chandelier, 1989).

Pam Conrad, *Balancing Home and Career: A Fifty-Minute Program* (Los Altos, Calif.: Crisp, 1990).

Susan B. Dynerman and Lynn O. Hayes, *The Best Jobs in America for Parents Who Want Careers and Time for Children Too* (New York: Rawson Associates, 1991).

Marcia E. Lasswell, *Equal Time: The New Way of Living, Loving, and Working Together* (Garden City, N.Y.: Doubleday, 1983).

CHAPTER 5

The Single Working Woman

The number of single-person households is projected to grow 20 percent between 1990 and 2010, according to *American Demographics'* projections.[1] The majority of working women are single. Some have never married and are career women on a fast track; some are widows, reluctantly plunged back into the workforce; and many are divorced women who never planned to be full-time working women. Most single women have no option about working. If there is to be bread on the table, they have to put it there. If there's to be a roof over their heads, they pay for it. Single women work in factories, in restaurants, and in support roles in every office in the country. They also head corporations and start their own businesses.

If there are any heroines today, they will be found among the ranks of single working mothers, who have to do everything as heads of households and who often have to act as both father and mother to their children. And they usually have to do it without the financial aid of the children's fathers, since most divorced fathers pay little or no child support.

Single women without children have the advantage of

Keep a positive attitude. Accept the things you can't change, and change the ones you can.

— Charlotte

being able to commit more of their time to their job. They are able to work long and flexible hours. These options put them far ahead of most of their married coworkers and especially ahead of single women with children. But the very advantages that put some single women ahead of married women can also be detrimental to their emotional, psychological, and physical well-being. It could be that they draw *too* much of their worth and personhood from what they do. If she is not careful, a single woman can find her life focusing mainly around her work. She has to fight against the temptation to let it be everything to her — to fill up the empty places in her life. The lifestyle of intense work, little play, and the inability to relax will definitely result in a stress-filled life.

It's not hard to find information about the working life of single working women. But it is difficult to find information about being a Christian and being single in the workplace. Let's take a look and see how a single working woman who is also a Christian can bring balance to her life.

I CAN FEEL GREAT!
I read somewhere a long time ago that one of the reasons for exhaustion may have nothing to do with the amount of work one is doing. It may well have to do with boredom, stress, and emotional drain. It's easy for a single woman to keep working, to never play — it takes so much effort to play.

If you're one of those who is constantly tired, it's time to take inventory and discover the cause. We need to discover and then deal with those things that cause us to live at what one young single mother calls "a poverty-mentality level." That poverty can be more than financial. It can be spiritual, emotional, physical, or even mental. Here are some questions to help you think about what's going on in your life.

- If I could do anything I wanted, what would it be?
- Am I making any progress toward my life goals?
- What is the one thing I'm doing that drains the emotional life out of me?
- How important to me is my relationship with God?
- How important to me is fellowship with other believers?
- Do I know about good nutrition, and do I eat properly?
- Do I exercise regularly?
- What do I do for recreation?
- Do I know how much sleep I need to function well?
- Do I get enough sleep?
- Do I relax when I'm doing some recreational activity, or do I pursue it in the same way I pursue my work?
- Am I overcommitted to social, church, or volunteer activities?
- How much time am I spending working at my job?
- Is my job the consuming factor in my life?
- Is it the primary source for my feelings of personal worth?

- Do all or most of my friends work at the same place?
- Are my housekeeping standards too high?
- Do I make time for those things that renew me — reading, journalizing, prayer, reflecting on life?
- Do I make time for family and/or special friends?
- Whom do I admire the most, and what qualities does that person have that cause me to admire him or her?

As a single working woman, I regularly have to ask myself these questions. They all boil down to one primary question: What's really important to me? Once that question is answered — and it's different for each person — we can begin to line things up in the order of their value.

I once had the most terrible case of stress-induced viral bronchitis imaginable. It went on for eight weeks. My sides ached from coughing and coughing and coughing. Along about the seventh week of the illness, I had a dental appointment. I wasn't sure I could hold my mouth open without coughing, so I asked the dentist if I should come in or wait. He encouraged me to come, and I'm glad he did because he taught me something that day that has helped me over and over again.

As I explained this lingering illness, he said to me, "Gwen, learn to listen to your body. It knows what it needs. It will heal itself when you give it what it needs. If you need to take time off work to rest and recuperate, do it. If you need to change jobs because of the stress, do it. Learn to listen."

We don't have to live life tired all the time. Begin to take steps to care for yourself, for your own sake and the sake of those your life impacts. Life was meant to be lived fully and richly. I believe that's what the Bible is talking about when it speaks of "abundant life."

Are you running from one social or volunteer activity to the next to fill up the hole of loneliness? It won't work. Each of us has to learn to be alone and to be content with our own company. That means we have to like ourselves and like our own company. It means we have to let God become our sufficiency.

Tough stuff, yes. But, oh the peace and satisfaction that come when we've learned the lesson. I suspect that the people you admire and want to spend time with are people who are content with themselves and have found a place of quiet within. We are all drawn to those people.

If low self-esteem is a problem area for you, consider seeing a counselor to help you sort out why you are trying to get your self-worth from what you do. Single women don't all have people in their lives to build their self-esteem. Many feel left out of life—as if they are lacking somehow. But it's not healthy to try to get our self-esteem from what or how much we do. God values us no matter what we do for a living. Search God's Word to find out what he thinks about your value. I can tell you he thinks you were a great idea.

Are you obsessive about a clean house? Why? Single people above all others can afford to be messy. Their mess doesn't impact anyone but themselves and their children, if they have children.

KEEP GOING FORWARD

All working women have to face the fact that from a compensation standpoint, we have not yet caught up with men. In a two-income household, that may not present much of a problem, but when a woman is on her own, it can be a *huge* problem.

Sandra Sanchez, writing in *USA Today,* says it will take women another thousand years to match the political and economic clout of men. Her information comes from a U.N. report put together by the International Labor Organization, which did a forty-one-nation survey and found that at the current rate of progress, women will

- hold equal managerial posts with men in 500 years
- reach equal political and economic status 475 years after that[2]

That's the sad truth that all working women must face. It isn't fair, and I think we owe it to ourselves and to future generations of working women to gently push the system. We have to remember that we are not just pushing to better ourselves but all those who will come after us.

So what do we do if we feel we are being discriminated against? We have to weigh all sides of the issue and decide what we, personally, are willing to pay to correct the problem. We may choose to deal with it by documentation and confrontation, but we have to be aware that our actions could bring further discrimination and even termination.

Not addressing the problem produces a seething mass inside that festers until it expresses itself in bitterness, anger, hatred, depression, or despair. It becomes toxic and destroys relationships or even causes illness. For me, that's too great a price to pay. So, to counteract the problem, I'm learning to confront in a fair, reasonable manner.

I've learned to preface my confrontational remarks with "I don't do this well, but I'm trying to learn how to confront without spewing my anger all over the place. Will you help me by telling me if what I'm saying is unfair or unfounded?" It's amazing how that question diffuses a potentially volatile situation. And I don't say it to manipulate the other person. I really mean that I'm still learning and someday I hope to do it better.

Remember, whether you are confronting the inequality of position or pay on the job or some relational problem, the goal is to achieve (to borrow a business phrase) a win/win situation. As women of grace and faith, we can't be out to "one-up" each other. We can't step on the next person to lift ourselves a little higher up the professional ladder. We have to seek solutions in which everyone wins — sometimes through compromise on everyone's part.

If you feel what's happening to you is unfair, deal with it either by confronting it, seeking God for the grace to put up with it, or walking away from the work situation that creates the unfairness. If you don't deal with the problem somehow, it will eat you alive from the inside out. And that's too great a price to pay.

*G*et active in organizations — professional and others. Stay active in church and singles groups. Go for more education. I know three women in their thirties who are getting college degrees. *—Lin*

I'M ALL I'VE GOT

It's true. And for some single women, like it or not, *I'm all I've got, and I may be all I'll ever have.* Whether our single situation is permanent or not, for now we're all we've got. Since this is true, it's vitally important to learn how to take care of ourselves.

Let's talk about pampering ourselves. What is it that makes you feel pampered? For me, in one town where I lived, it was a croissant and café au lait in a French-style restaurant on Saturday mornings. A pianist with unbelievable talent came in to entertain the breakfasters. What's your idea of pampering? Here are some ideas to get you started:

- A hot bubble bath
- A cup of tea beside the fire
- A walk in the forest
- Dinner with a friend
- A drive in the country
- A shopping spree
- A ski trip
- A swim in a lake
- Time in a hot tub
- A new bottle of perfume
- A fluffy comforter
- New underwear
- A bouquet of flowers for your desk
- A long chat on the phone with a good friend

FIND MOMENTS OF WONDER

They can be big expensive things or little simple times or

places that bring us pleasure. In her book *Pilgrim at Tinker Creek*, Annie Dillard tells about becoming quiet within and learning to observe what is right around us. Annie speaks in that book of "moments of wonder." I have trained myself to look for moments of wonder every day. I find that these moments give me great pleasure. May I indulge myself and share a couple with you?

I live in the woods at an elevation of seventy-five hundred feet. The other day I was sitting at my computer when I saw something coming up through the woods. At first I thought it was a cat, but then I saw that it was a red fox. He didn't know I was watching him, so he lay down in the snow and began grooming himself. He was not more than thirty feet away. At last something frightened him, and he ran off—his long black stockings pumping up and down and his fluffy red tail trailing straight out behind.

Several mornings I have awakened to find the pine trees and everything else flocked with hoarfrost. The last time, it was so thick that it made a pencil-sized branch as big as a broomstick. When I came home in the evening, the fog that had caused the frost was still hanging about, but the snow-white trees filled the moonlit landscape.

The next morning the sun was shining, and I knew the hoarfrost would be gone in a matter of minutes. But once again, as I drove to work, I saw something I'd never seen before. The trees dropped the frost around themselves in a circular pattern. There were circles of white under every tree. They looked like they had shrugged out of gossamer gowns and let them slide to the ground.

Oh, and there have been other moments, like seeing five geese flying just above the pines, or the patter of little

*D*on't wait for Mr. Right to come along and bail you out! Build a support network: Join a support or recovery group, special interest group, Bible study, etc. —*Alison*

squirrel feet on my roof, or intensely blue Steller's jays feeding at my bird feeder, or a funny-looking black squirrel with tufted ears hurrying on his way, or what I see right now, a squirrel hanging precariously on a tiny limb, cutting pieces for his new spring nest.

The world is full of wonder, and if we learn to listen, smell, taste, feel, and see, there is so much to bring us pleasure.

FIND SOMEONE TO LOVE

And then there's love. Everyone needs to love and be loved. Being single is no excuse for not loving and being loved. What kind of people do you need to be loved by or to love?

Some women enjoy older people. They love to learn of their wisdom. They love to hear the stories of their struggles and victories. It gives younger women hope.

Other women, like me, need children. Mine are grown now. I have no grandchildren, so I spend time with young families who have small children. I don't know how those children view me—as some kind of aunt or something, I suppose. I only know a beautiful thing grows inside when I'm holding a tiny girl in my arms, reading her a story.

Just last Sunday one of those tiny girls, Annie, handed me a picture she'd drawn for me. It had Mommy, Daddy, Annie, and Gwen in the picture. My heart nearly burst with love.

Some women love animals. We're told animals are good for us, that when you pet an animal your blood pressure drops. I have lived with animals a good portion of my adult life but recently had to say good-bye to a four-legged friend of mine because she was ill. I realized I was not home enough for her, and I probably could not be for any animal, so I have made the difficult decision not to have a pet right now. It's the right decision, but it's hard because I do enjoy the companionship of a pet.

But beyond kids and animals, there are lots of places to show love. Hospices need volunteers to sit with the dying. Various ministries and nonprofit agencies need people to staff hot lines. These are all acts of love that cannot help but bring joy to our lives.

And we must not forget the church. This is still a place where growth and nurturing of individuals takes place. Most church education programs are understaffed. Pastors would be ecstatic if single people would devote a couple of hours a week to helping with the educational programs. In a church where I was once associated, about half the children's programs were staffed by single people. Those singles were influencing lives for the future. They were giving love, and they were loved. Remember, though, to evaluate your strength, time, and energy before committing to help out at church.

YOU'RE NOT ALONE

I know it feels like it. But about one-third of the population is single. There is strength in numbers, and it is important to find a support network. It can be a singles group at your church, a group of women friends who meet periodically just to enjoy one another, a group of working mothers with common concerns, or just several individual friends who will be there for you when you need someone to turn to. It is very appealing to be needed by someone.

Several years ago I went into a counseling program to straighten out some confusion in my life. The first thing my counselor said to me was "How many support people do you have in your life?" I could think of about three. She said, "That's not enough. You need at least twenty people."

I just sat and looked at her. How was I going to get twenty people to support me? But she had the answer to my unvoiced question. She said, "People may like you and may want to be there for you, but they can't know what's going on in your life until you tell them. You have to reach out to them and say, 'I need you.'"

Where do you find those people? Some of them are the people with whom you work. Some are in the church you attend. Some you may meet at social gatherings. Some are in your family.

The reason for having twenty such people is so that when you truly need a friend, someone will be available. I've found that the best people for this role are those who have themselves been through whatever it is you're going through—those who have been in need, have been working through their pain, have struggled financially, or whatever else you're facing. For especially challenging situations, you may even want to join an organized support group, such as those in twelve-step programs or other counseling situations.

I've learned so much about friendship from the people in my support network. One friend said, "If you need me, I'm here. You can call me any time of day or night, and you don't have to say a word. You can just cry if you want." I didn't think I'd ever need to take advantage of her offer, but one day I did. That's love, that's friendship, and now it's my turn to be there for my friends.

When I relocated to Colorado Springs, I only knew five people in the town. I knew what I had to do, and I began actively cultivating friendships. I invited people in for dinner even though I didn't have a dining room table. I had a group in for a video night. I had families come, and we spent the afternoon sledding together. I accepted invitations to visit them at the drop of a hat. I joined friends in restaurants on the spur of the moment. I went hiking with some active young people. I found a church and started showing up regularly and getting to know people. I joined professional organizations. Some of my friends put together a book-reading club, and we learned not only about books, but also about each other. Building friendships is an ongoing process for me; after several years, it's coming along.

Reach out and say, in words or in actions, "I need your friendship." Chances are you'll find it.

KIDS, VACATIONS, AND SICK LEAVE

A couple of years ago I was talking with the owner of a day-care center about the needs of single working mothers. She was expressing great dismay over the fact that many single working mothers bring their children to the day-care center when they are ill. And I don't just mean sniffles and a runny nose — I mean a fever and lethargy.

It's tough to be the single mother of a sick child. Sick children need their mothers. They need to be loved and held. But they also need a roof over their heads and food on the table, and Mom simply has to work to provide them.

There are only a few facilities in the country that will care for sick children in a day-care situation. It's not hard to understand how disease can sweep through a day-care center. It's not always easy on the day-care workers, either. My daughter managed to avoid chicken pox all her life until a couple of years ago when she was working in a day-care center. She caught it from the kids, and she was a pretty sick day-care worker.

Single mothers of children too young to be left on their own when they are sick need to hang on to their sick time for emergencies like this. If your company doesn't allow the use of sick time to care for a sick child, then you may need to save a chunk of personal or vacation time for this purpose. You also need some kind of backup plan: a sitter who will take sick children or a friend or family member who will help out in an emergency. Here again, a network of friends can help you survive in the event of a child's emergency illness.

There is a program in Colorado Springs that is wonderful for employees who have run out of sick time for whatever reason. City employees are allowed to donate vacation time to other employees. That way, when an employee or an employee's child has an extended illness, the paychecks keep coming in. The idea was conceived and pushed through by city employees. "Under the program employees can donate Personal Annual Leave or PAL time to a Penrose-St. Francis [hospital] bank. The time can be accrued vacation days, sick leave, personal days and bereavement allotments. Then, employees who need additional time for illness or other emergencies may apply to the foundation to receive the time."[3]

This is a practical and lovely idea that deserves to be spread throughout the land. Perhaps it is something to propose to the company for which you work. All good ideas have to start somewhere, and you might be the one to start a program that benefits fellow employees.

And what about being single and taking vacations? An extended time of rest is vital to anyone's well-being. Singles need it as much as anybody. For most of us, it takes several days to unwind so that we can enjoy our time of rest. So a "real" vacation is in order.

But where do single working women go on vacation, and with whom? (Chapter 14 has lots of information about travel for both married and single working women and for singles with children.)

I have a friend, an extremely resourceful single lady, who just got back from New York City. She used frequent flyer coupons and award coupons from hotels and went to New York by herself. She saw three or four plays, ate at a couple of good restaurants, and came home—refreshed, happy.

Another friend, a single mom, has her daughter in a private school, so funds for play are limited. But here is another resourceful woman. She made arrangements for her daughter

Get involved with others. Be a friend, not only to singles, but also to couples with children and to the elderly. Take someone's children for a day or two and enjoy them. Have friends of both sexes. —Karen

to attend camp in the Ozarks for free. In exchange, she was a camp counselor. They drove over from Colorado to Missouri, which gave them quality time together, and spent the week there. It was such a successful experience that the camp is now offering similar scholarships to the children of other single parents.

I have another single working friend who last summer finally got the courage to take a vacation that did not include several days at her parents' house. She says the experience of doing something else was wonderful. As we all know, being single is not equal to being immature, so there's no reason why a single adult must check in with her parents every year—unless that's what she wants to do.

A great idea for single women is to travel together. When you take a friend on a trip, you can share the expenses (as well as the driving, if traveling by car). Of course, the person you travel with must be compatible with your travel style, and you have to learn the rules of traveling with a friend. For instance, I learned that I didn't have the right to be the tour guide and arrange every detail of a joint adventure. My friend had some ideas, too, and hers were as valid and exciting as mine.

Some churches arrange group travel activities for singles. This seems to work well, particularly for older singles. But if you are going to travel with a group of any kind, you will have to wait for someone—plan on it. In Europe I've stumbled over tons of luggage sitting on the sidewalk outside a hotel: the evidence of a tour group awaiting late tour members so they could begin the day's activities.

But the benefits of traveling with a group are meeting wonderful people, having companionship, and saving money (tours are usually less expensive than traveling on your own). Tour companies know which sights are worth seeing and have special passes to get into attractions. That means you'll probably see more in the time you have available. Touring is definitely an attractive option for single people.

LIVE NOW

I guess if I have a closing word for single working women it would be that they *live now*. I've worked with singles and taught classes for them for years. During those years I've watched singles — particularly women — and I think there's a strong tendency to delay life. Some are waiting to live until they are married, or have more money, or until they retire.

But we're only going to live once, so my advice is to live now.

I remember a woman whose church choir was traveling to Australia, and she wanted to go. But the only way she could do it was to quit her job — and it was an excellent job. I don't know why she asked my advice, but she did. Since she was young and very talented in her work, and since this was a once-in-a-lifetime opportunity, I told her to risk it and go — to live now.

While such drastic action is not for everyone, she went and has never been sorry. She came back and found a better job. She finished college by going to night classes and pretty soon bought a lovely home.

Not only are we all we've got, but the only time we have is now. So *live now!*

SUGGESTED READING

Dandi D. Knorr, *Just One of Me: Confessions of a Less-than-Perfect Single Parent* (Wheaton, Ill.: Harold Shaw, 1989).

Karen S. Linamen and Linda Holland, *Working Women, Workable Lives: Creative Solutions for Managing Home and Career* (Wheaton, Ill.: Harold Shaw, 1993).

Mary Whelchel, *The Christian Working Woman* (Grand Rapids: Baker, 1988).

CHAPTER 6

The Primary Caregiver

Our national child-care problems were catapulted onto the front pages of our newspapers when two candidates for the position of attorney general of the United States were rejected because of child-care/tax-related problems. Zoe Baird and Kimba Woods are working mothers who found it essential to hire child-care workers. Zoe Baird, at least, failed to pay the required taxes—Social Security, Medicare, and unemployment—to the government. Even though she made it right—paid the back taxes and fees—the damage was done. She was disqualified from being a candidate for this most prestigious legal position. The job finally went to a single, childless woman.

Ask any working mother about the problem, and be prepared to listen for a long time while she pours out her heart, not just about child care, but also about the growing problem of how to care for her aging parents. A recent morning television show reported that the number of people eighty-five years of age and older has quadrupled in the last few years. It also stated that one in five workers will soon be caring for an aging parent.[1] Perhaps no part of the

My husband is available [for child care] most of the time when I'm working. In addition to that I have a network of adult sitters I can use. —Adelyn

working woman's life is as difficult and as important to her as that of being the primary caregiver for either dependent children or aging parents. Life is truly complicated for the working woman who has both responsibilities.

I know we've all heard the saying that working women are the sandwich generation. One slice of the bread is our young children who must be cared for, and the other slice of bread is our aging parents, who also need our attention and care. And we are the bologna in the middle. Sometimes we feel that way, don't we?

How Can I Find Adequate Child Care?
An ongoing question working mothers ask is, How can I find adequate child care? Sometimes working women feel all alone in their quest for quality care—but you're not alone. Every day 23 million children are cared for in a child-care arrangement.[2] Did you know that this year American families will spend upward of $30 billion on child care and the government will spend $9 billion?[3] Thirty-nine billion dollars! That's a lot of baby-sitting!

I work in a large organization that employs many single mothers. Most of them struggle from time to time with child-care problems. As long as a baby-sitter is available and the child stays well, things go pretty well for the working mom. But when a child becomes ill, many baby-sitters, day-care centers, and other caregivers will not take the child. These caregivers are not trying to be cruel; it just makes sense. They don't want a raging epidemic in the center.

That means a single mom has to either take time off from work or find individual care for the child. Married mothers have the same problem, except that in their case there is another caregiver in the family. Sometimes Dad can juggle his schedule to be there for the sick child. Between the two of them, they are sometimes able to manage the caregiving crisis.

Eleanor and Dick, both junior high school teachers, take turns staying home when one of their two children is sick. "We take these as our own sick days," says Eleanor. "Fortunately, we're healthy, so we have enough leeway to take off for our kids' runs of colds and sore throats. What I can't understand, though, is why a school, which is concerned with the welfare of children, doesn't have an official policy of letting parents stay home to take care of their own children."

In her book *The Working Parents Survival Guide*, author Sally Wendkos Olds says:

> The jobs most people hold do not encourage them to be good parents. To the contrary, they generally seem to be in direct conflict. The hours are often long and rigidly defined. There is pressure to complete the work in hand immediately, no matter what the home situation. No provision is made for taking time off for family-related reasons such as a child's illness or performance in a school play. Parents often feel guilty

about spending time with their children. When they do feel they have to take time off from work, they feel forced to lie about the reasons.[4]

Then there are summers. What does a child do for an entire summer while Mom works? My friend Deb is one of the most resourceful single moms I've ever met. She starts months ahead of summer to line up activities for her daughter, Jamie.

A recent *American Demographics* article said, "The hardest part about being a mother hasn't changed; it is family demands. . . . When asked 'Which of the following worries you the most because of the demands of your job — job will suffer; children will suffer; marriage will suffer; none; or all,' 51 percent say none. Almost one-third (32 percent) fear that their children will suffer, 8 percent say that their marriage will suffer, 3 percent say their job will suffer, and 4 percent say all will suffer."[5] Probably the reason that 32 percent are concerned for their children is directly related to finding adequate child care. Not to bore you with statistics, but 58 percent of women in the workforce are women with children under six years of age.[6] Now it doesn't take a nuclear physicist to figure out that with statistics like this, we have a huge child-care problem in this country.

The president has signed the family leave bill after many years of debate. I don't think the debate has ever been over whether we want to care for our children or not; it was a concern over whether small businesses could survive employees' taking up to twelve weeks of leave for birth, adoption, or family medical emergencies with continued health benefits. Even though the employer would not be paying wages (only health benefits), he would probably have to hire a temporary worker to replace the employee. What happens to a business that has to keep a position open for an employee who is not working?

We are just finding that out at our office. One of our secretaries is having a baby, and we can hardly wait for the child to be born. She has opted to take the full twelve weeks' leave before making her decision about returning to work. And while everyone is excited for her, we are struggling with how we are going to cope during her absence. We will be using a temporary worker to fill in the gap, and none of us thinks that is going to be very easy.

What's interesting to me is that several other countries already have family leave policies for parental or maternity leave. In Canada an employee gets fifteen weeks at 60 percent pay, in Sweden thirty-eight weeks at 90 percent pay, in Finland thirty-five weeks at 100 percent pay, in Germany fourteen to nineteen weeks at 100 percent pay, in Austria twenty weeks at 100 percent pay, in Italy twenty-two weeks at 80 percent pay, in France sixteen weeks at 90 percent pay, and in Japan twelve weeks at 60 percent pay.[7] So the United States has hardly been a leader when it comes to child care and family leave. Perhaps that will change with the signing of the family leave bill.

WHERE DO KIDS GO WHEN MOM WORKS?
Many are dropped off at church day-care centers, child-care centers set down in the middle of strip malls, centers that are part of a nationwide franchise operation, or child-care centers set up in homes. The quality of care children receive can vary as much as the kinds of child-care centers.

A lot of kids—49 percent, one source says—are cared for either full-time or after school by another relative.

Family day care is another option. This is different from the day-care center in someone's home. This is the kind of care where your child joins a family. Most parents like this arrangement because the child receives more personalized attention in such a setting.

A more expensive alternative is an in-home baby-sitter or nanny. Baby-sitters are usually in the home only during the hours the parents are working. A nanny often lives in the house and has other responsibilities besides child care. While she has regular working hours, she may be called on for additional child care in the evenings as well. Only 4 percent of working mothers use this type of care.

The YMCA is a leader in after-school care: care during the hours between school and the time the parent gets off work. Since after-school programs are usually structured, they can be a valuable learning experience for the child.

Some employers are recognizing that child care is a major family issue and are beginning to provide on-site child-care facilities. But the percentage is still small, only 13 percent. More companies are helping out with referral services, which help their employees learn about various day-care options in their community.[8]

Sometimes small companies are more flexible and therefore better places for parents of young children to work. Small companies, which may not have the ability to provide on-site day care or even offer a monetary benefit for employees, may be able to offer options such as flextime, job sharing, and allowing an employee to work at home. Perhaps parents of young children should search out these companies as places of employment.

Bev is in a flextime situation. She is a crackerjack publicist and the mother of a young child. She leaves Ben with a baby-sitter in the morning while she goes to her office to take care of routine work and get her secretary started on projects, then she works at home in the afternoons. He sleeps part of that time, and she is able to continue working while he sleeps. She fits the rest of her hours around the other tasks of caring for him. Sometimes she has to work into the evening hours after her husband comes home, but she tries to avoid that. The main things are that she does her job well and that the child is being adequately cared for.

Now another child is on the way, and Bev has decided it is going to be too complicated to continue working outside the home. When this baby is born, she will quit and open a home office from which she will do publicity work for a number of publishing companies.

If your company does nothing else to help, it can, perhaps, offer a dependent-care-assistance plan (DCAP). This allows parents on the payroll to set aside tax-free dollars (up to five thousand dollars a year) to pay for child care. This is one of the least expensive things a company can do. (For more information, ask your company to request the DCAP Handbook from the Massachusetts Public Interest Re-

I am in constant communication with my daughter's caregivers. That gives them and my child the message that she is important to me, and it also lends an additional accountability factor. —Deb

search Group Education Fund, 29 Temple Place, Boston, MA 02111, phone 617-292-4800.)

Good, caring companies in the nineties will want to be progressive along with their competitors and to do what's best for their employees. Challenge your personnel department to investigate and find ways to help with this crucial employment problem. I've done this and found a listening ear.

WHAT'S AHEAD IN CHILD CARE?

For a while child care is going to go along pretty much the way it has. But there will be some small changes. They will be:

- More companies will offer full-time day-care facilities to their employees as part of a benefits program.
- More people with babies and small children will use in-home care, where only two or three infants or toddlers are cared for at one time.
- Public schools will begin to offer part-day prekindergarten and other programs.
- There will be consideration of year-round schools. This will do away with the need for extended summer child care, but it might also create the problem of several two- to three-week periods throughout the year when child care is needed.
- There's talk about financing a child-care system in the same way we finance our public school system, by taxing all citizens. It's not a bad idea if we truly believe that our children are our future.
- There will probably be sick-child services. There may be facilities established for this purpose, but

more likely companies will offer additional personal days for this purpose.[9]

LATCHKEY KIDS

Here is a problem that won't go away: kids who have to be home alone while parents work. Most of these children are between the ages of eight and fifteen. These children are from all socioeconomic levels; in fact, recent studies indicate that children of parents with a higher education are more likely to be self-care kids.[10]

Different children are ready for self-care at different ages. There is no magical age at which children are ready to be on their own. It is a decision only a parent can make.

One of the biggest problems parents have to face is feeling guilty about leaving their child alone. And some children are smart enough to use your guilt for their own purposes — "If you'd been home this wouldn't have happened." One way to handle the guilt is to admit that although you work, and although your child has to be alone for a few hours each day, you can still provide a positive home environment. Learn to recognize whether you feel false guilt — because you are not doing it the way your parents did or because some other external pressure is making you feel guilty — or whether you are really doing something wrong. Assess what it is that makes you worry.

- What could you do to make you feel better about the problem?
- What fears do you have?

*I*f you can't afford day care, the Department of Human Services in your city has a program to pay for you — or assist you, depending on your income. With children fourteen and older, there are work programs to keep them busy and also earning spending money.

— Joyce

- Do you feel you are doing a good job as a parent? Why or why not?
- How do your children feel about your working?

There can be some real positives for the self-care child. He can learn to do tasks and take responsibility in a way children whose moms are there to do everything for them never do. Some children like to take care of themselves. They are proud of their ability to cope.

It's important to get the child to tell you how he feels about self-care. Is he one that really likes it, or is he one that is upset and frightened most of the time he's alone? Try to get at the child's true feelings. Some children act like it's all right because they think that will please you, when they truly hate being alone.

A marvelous book, *Alone after School: A Self-Care Guide for Latchkey Children and Their Parents,* by Helen Swan and Victoria Houston, covers just about every possible aspect of self-care. It provides information and checklists for safety, loneliness, fear, injuries, handling your own guilt, knowing when a child is ready to be alone after school, and how to make the time you have together quality time. I highly recommend the book, which is listed along with other books on the subject at the end of this chapter.

Sometimes there are no options but to leave an older child alone for a few hours after school. It's tough, but it's true. It doesn't mean you're a failure as a parent, and it can be a tremendously profitable time for the child. As with most things in life, a good attitude about the problem and a willingness to find solutions that work for both you and the child are important.

THE OTHER END OF THE SPECTRUM

Because the American population is aging quickly, many working women have or will soon have another problem — that of caring for aging parents. Estimates are that one in five American workers is currently caring for an aging parent, and that number grows every year.

We've all heard about the "mommy track," but now a new phrase has been coined. It's called the "daughter track," and it simply means that more and more women are having to take a slower track of career development because of caring for aging parents.

This has not been a big problem for most people in the past, and it is a medium-sized problem now, but in the very near future it's going to become a huge problem. In 1987, 29.8 million Americans were older than 65 — 12.3 percent of the population. Just three years later, in 1990, according to the U.S. Census Bureau, there were over 31 million persons 65 and older, which was 12.6 percent of the population. By 2050 it is estimated there will be over 68 million older people, who will make up 23 percent of the total population. By 2050 more than 5 percent of the population will be over 85.[11]

If you are in the middle of the dilemma that comes with caring for aging parents while trying to maintain some semblance of family life and normality for yourself, you are not alone. It is estimated that 6 million elderly Americans need help with such basics as getting out of bed or going to the bathroom. Many more are unable to prepare meals, handle money transactions, or get where they need to go on their own.

Consider yourself a caregiver if you have an elderly person living in your home who is in any way disabled or chronically ill. The time you spend caregiving may only be a few hours a week, or it may be an extensive amount of time. In addition to helping the elderly person from bed or to the bathroom, you may also be cooking, cleaning, giving shots or other medications, changing dressings and intravenous tubes, handling finances, running errands, and providing comfort both to the elderly person and to other members of the family.

Caregiving in the home happens first of all because the caregiver loves the parent or older person and wants him to have the best care possible. Second, the expense of caring for an older person in a facility outside the home often makes it essential to give care in the home.

Most of us come to caregiving unprepared for it. Two of the things I'd like to do are make you aware that this can happen to you and help you prepare for that eventuality. The onset of caregiving can be abrupt—occurring literally overnight. One day Mom is fine, and the next day a stroke renders her incapacitated. Be aware that within each community there are agencies and people to train you to make caring for an older person a reward and not an unending burden. While it may seem that you are the only person who has ever tried to cope with caring for an elderly parent, you are not. Make use of a support group, professional expertise, and helping agencies.

By the time a parent or other older person needs full-time care, the situation can be so critical that it is very stressful both for the caregiver and for the dependent person. Most older people have lived proud, independent lives, and suddenly they are helpless and uprooted from their own surroundings. They may be confused, angry, and afraid.

Just about the time a working woman has her children launched and thinks she's going to be able to have some leisure time to herself, she has to begin caring for her parents. And because people now live so long, she may even be caring for her grandparents. Don't fool yourself; although many men are helping more than ever before, still three-fourths of those caring for aging parents are women. The fact that many women are now employed outside their homes hasn't changed the mentality about their caregiving role very much, and it is still mostly women who care for the family's aged.

It isn't very encouraging, but it is the truth that most of us will spend more time caring for our parents than we did for our children. It's a discomforting statistic that won't go away, and we must not ignore it. We must, instead, plan for the time when we will be full-time caregivers to our parents.

If you think it's difficult to ask for time off to help your child, try asking for time off to take care of your mother. Once again, the demands on an employee's sick time and vacation time are enormous. Employees use these days to take their elderly parent to the doctor or shopping or to care for them in some other way. Most employees with an aging parent really have two full-time jobs: the one they're paid to do and the one they do the rest of the time—shopping, handling Medicare papers, visiting the parent, or doing the myriad of other things parents cannot do on their own.

Companies that are helping employees with aging parents are almost nil. They are only about 3 percent. The passage of the Family and Medical Leave Act of 1993 should give some relief for workers with aging parents because the rule that applies to child care also applies to care of other family members: Twelve weeks off without pay are given to care for newborn or adopted children or *relatives* who are seriously ill.

It's interesting that feminist groups, who are so quick to speak out about injustices to working women, have not been quick to consider the problem of caregiving; and yet it is probably the biggest concern of working women. No matter what else they talk about, working women come back again and again to the concerns of caregiving. It impacts everything else they do.

One of the biggest dangers for any caregiver is that of burnout. I'm always fascinated by the instructions given on an airplane—to put on your own oxygen mask before you help someone else. What that says is you can't help someone else if you're unconscious. It's the same in caregiving. You can't help someone else if you're burned-out and have nothing left to give. You owe it to yourself and your loved ones to eat properly, get regular exercise, and take breaks from your caregiving responsibilities. *No one is going to take care of you but you.* That's one fact you can count on.

Since caregiving is a full-time job all by itself, get help for the other areas of your life that don't matter so much. It's all right to hire someone to clean your house. It's all right to put your parent in an adult day-care center if you can find one. It's all right to have someone in to cook your meals. It's all right if someone brings meals in to your parent while you're away at work. It's all right to turn over some of your responsibilities to others. It's all right if eventually you have to place your parent in a nursing home or hospital.

Some women can't cope with it all and decide the only thing they can do is to quit their jobs and care for their parents full-time. They believe it is a less expensive route in the long run than trying to keep a job and paying someone else to do the caregiving. Whichever way working women decide—working and caregiving simultaneously or taking care of an elderly parent full-time—there is a price to be paid.

Whatever you decide, it's important not to wait to seek support help. The earlier you have support, the less chance there is that you will burn out. If you have aging parents, give some thought to the information presented here. Then when the crisis comes, you'll be ready for it.

I use a caregiver from my church when I'm substitute teaching. I work at a school in the neighborhood, so I'm home when our seven-year-old arrives from school.   —*Carol*

A PLAN OF ACTION
If you have an aging parent, you can

begin to get ready for the caregiving time. Here are some suggestions:

- Look in the telephone directory for caregiving organizations.
- Look for those that provide home health care, assistance with household chores, financial and legal assistance, and recreational activities.
- Contact the local city or county office on aging.
- Contact the health department.
- Contact senior centers.
- Contact the Veterans Administration if that is applicable.
- Check out Meals on Wheels.
- Determine if the American Red Cross provides support in your area.
- See if the American Alzheimer's Association has an office in your area.
- Check to see what other facilities and agencies are available.
- Call these agencies and get their literature. *Read it.*
- Visit day-care facilities, nursing homes, senior citizens' centers, and other agencies to see what they are like.
- Take your elderly parents to visit these centers and agencies. Begin to prepare them for the time when they will be a part of these programs.

RESOURCES TO HELP WITH CHILD CARE
- Parents in the United States can get a tax credit of up to $1440 annually for child care.

- Child Care Action Campaign, Dept. P, 330 Seventh Ave., New York, NY 10001.
- *Working Moms, Caring and Sharing* is a quarterly newsletter for Christian working moms. Contact them at P.O. Box 2413, Yakima, WA 98907-2413. The subscription price is $6.95 per year with a special two-year rate. When you subscribe, you will receive a free copy of a booklet called *Reader Write-In Questions & Answers* and information about networking opportunities. The newsletter is packed with information of value to working mothers.

RESOURCES TO HELP WITH ELDER CARE

- Alzheimer's Disease and Related Disorders, Chicago, phone 800-272-3900
- American Association of Homes for the Aging, 1129 20th St. NW, Suite 400, Edina, MN 55435
- American Association of Retired People (AARP), 601 E Street NW, Washington, DC 20049, phone 202-434-2277. The AARP has the following free booklets available: *A Path for Caregivers, Making Wise Decisions for Long-Term Care, A Profile of Older Americans, Before You Buy: A Guide to Long-Term Care Insurance, The Financial Impact of Multiple Family Responsibilities on Midlife and Older People, Medigap: Medicare Supplement Insurance, Health Care Power of Attorney,* and *The Social Security Book.*
- As Parents Grow Older, Institute of Gerontology,

*T*ry to hire outside help to allow [elderly parents] to remain independent — use Meals on Wheels, etc.   —*Nancy*

University of Michigan, Ann Arbor, MI 48109
- Children of Aging Parents (CAPS), 1609 Woodbourne Road, Suite 302A, Levittown, PA 19057, Phone 215-345-5104

SUGGESTED READING ON CHILD CARE

Earl Grollman, *Teaching Your Child to Be Home Alone* (New York: Free Press, 1992).

Elsa Houtz, *The Working Mother's Guide to Sanity* (Eugene, Oreg.: Harvest House, 1989).

Dandi D. Knorr, *Just One of Me: Confessions of a Less-than-Perfect Single Parent,* (Wheaton, Ill.: Harold Shaw, 1989).

Karen S. Linamen and Linda Holland, *Working Women, Workable Lives: Creative Solutions for Managing Home and Career* (Wheaton, Ill.: Harold Shaw, 1993).

Sally W. Olds, *The Working Parent's Survival Guide* (Rocklin, Calif.: Prima, 1989).

Ellie R. Peters, *Home Child Care: The Tender Business* (South Bend, Ind.: Greenlawn, 1990).

Bryan E. Robinson, *Home Alone Kids: Working Parent's Guide to Providing the Best Care for Your Child* (Lexington, Mass.: Free Press, 1990).

Carolyn Sedgwick, *When Mothers Must Work* (Springdale, Penn.: Whitaker House, 1988).

Helen L. Swan and Victoria Houston, *Alone after School: A Self-Care Guide for Latchkey Children and Their Parents* (Englewood, N.J.: Prentice Hall, 1987).

SUGGESTED READING ON ELDER CARE

Barbara Deane, *Caring for Your Aging Parents* (Colorado Springs: NavPress, 1989).

Nancy L. Mace and Peter V. Rabins, *The Thirty-Six-Hour Day: A Family Guide to Caring for Persons with Alzheimer's Disease, Related Dementing Illnesses, and Memory Loss in Later Life* (New York: Warner Books, 1992).

Robert J. Riekse and Henry Holstege, *The Christian Guide to Parent Care* (Wheaton, Ill.: Tyndale House, 1992).

Kerri S. Smith, *Caring for Your Aging Parents: A Sourcebook of Timesaving Techniques and Tips* (Lakewood, Colo.: American Source Books, 1992).

Todd Temple and Tracy Green, *Fifty-Two Ways to Show Aging Parents You Care* (Nashville: Nelson, 1992).

CHAPTER 7

The Harried Cook

It seems that advertising tells us more about who we are than we like to admit. One recent ad said, "Around here, the homemaker is anybody who happens to be home. Ring a doorbell today, and it's likely a teenager will answer with an armful of laundry. Or a dad in a sauce-stained apron. This is life. Because these days, women aren't busy just in the home. . . ."

When I sent out my survey to working women, many busy women found time to answer, and some of them gave real insight into just how busy a working woman's life can be.

"Thanks so much for including me in your survey," said Marie. "I laid your letter on the kitchen counter, and to-night between fixing supper, doing dishes, baking cookies, and starting tomorrow's supper, I jotted down answers to your questions. If some of them seem fragmented, it's be-cause I added to my answers after I thought about them a while."

It sounds to me as if Marie has the cooking thing pretty much under control, but others who answered the survey either left the question blank or admitted they have no plan for meal preparation. Others said that their families eat out a

I plan the whole week's meals ahead. I do most of my cooking the evening I shop and try to chop veggies, make meatballs, etc., then, too.   *—Marie*

lot. And I wondered how families can afford to eat out on a regular basis. It seems all of the profits from working would quickly be "eaten" up.

A number of other respondents said they had a plan. Many of them said they cook in bulk one or two days a week. Since cooking in bulk is a good, efficient plan for working women, we'll talk more about it later in this chapter.

Life is not the same as it was when our grandmothers were homemakers and could spend hours preparing a favorite meal. Now children and/or a husband have to get involved in the kitchen to make the system work well. I don't think that's detrimental. I know too many men who never learned to boil water and are completely helpless in the kitchen. It began when they were children, and they were either not allowed in the kitchen or discouraged from being there. Children, both boys and girls, need to learn the basics of cooking for their own future and because you need their help now. Husbands who never had a chance to learn how to cook might find it a tremendously creative venture. After all, most of the great chefs of the world are men.

THE IMPORTANCE OF FOOD

My dad is eighty years old. He's a meat-and-potatoes kind of guy, and he's put away a lot of them in his life. He has a philosophy about food and weight control that I now hear being espoused more and more by nutritionists and medical people. He believes that people have to eat well to stay well. We have to take in enough calories to nourish and strengthen our bodies so that they can work. Weight should be controlled by physical exercise and work. We put calories into our bodies, and we burn them up. Our bodies have the benefit of extracting what they need in terms of minerals, vitamins, protein, amino acids, etc., from the wide range of foods we eat.

Too many people today are doing just the opposite. They are cutting back on calories, which makes them too weak to work and exercise effectively. Then their metabolism gets all out of whack, and even though they are going around hungry, they continue to gain weight.

Food is important and necessary to our bodies. It's fuel. That's why God gave us an appetite. You know everything within your body is working the way it's supposed to when you have a good appetite. Someone who is terminally ill loses his appetite and has to be force-fed or struggles to get a few bites down. Be thankful for a good appetite.

Too many people, working women being among the worst offenders, skip breakfast and start the day with inadequate nutrition. We need something to *break* our all-night *fast*. It's a proven fact that children who have had breakfast are better able to concentrate. That's why some schools provide a breakfast meal for underprivileged children.

Some of us are treating ourselves like underprivileged children. Hungry workers don't think and perform well either. We don't outgrow our need for breakfast, and it's important that we take time to get something into ourselves and our family members before we all head out the door.

People under stress generally either eat excessively or stop eating. "The overeater's blood is diverted from the brain to the stomach, and the undereater deprives her brain of essential nutrients."[1] The fatty foods we tend to gravitate to for a pick-me-up when we are under stress—candy bars, donuts—only worsen the situation. And furthermore, Joan Horbiak, president and founder of the Health and Nutrition Network, says that a change in diet can help keep stress under control.

You can see what you might be doing to yourself if you are starting the day with either nothing in your stomach or by consuming sugary, fatty foods.

SO, WHAT SHALL WE DO ABOUT BREAKFAST?

Breakfast doesn't have to be terribly elaborate to serve its purpose. Nonsugared prepared cereals—shredded wheat, bran flakes, low-fat granola—are easy to prepare and quick to eat. Spoon on some low-fat yogurt or fresh fruit for added taste and nutrition.

Why not keep some frozen whole wheat waffles in the freezer? Toast them in the toaster. Heat a little low-calorie syrup or honey in the microwave. It only takes two minutes to prepare this breakfast.

Learn to eat whole grain cereals—oatmeal, cooked cracked wheat, seven-grain cereals, etc.—and teach your kids to eat them, too. These take about fifteen minutes to cook, but once you get the water boiling and dump the cereal into it, you can turn the heat off and get ready for work. By the time you've applied your makeup, the cereal is ready. Sprinkle on some raisins and a little milk, and you have a tasty, nutritious, and very inexpensive breakfast.

As you know, you can also buy frozen breakfasts. But before you do, take a look at the label. Such items as eggs, sausage, and ham can push your cholesterol level sky-high. The all-American breakfast can be a killer.

Of course, there are all kinds of wonderful breads for toast; there are muffins, bagels, English muffins, Australian toaster biscuits, and tons of other baked goods. A bit of bread and a little jam, jelly, or honey do a good job of breaking a fast.

You can even go nontraditional and spread a little pizza sauce on an English muffin, add some cheese, maybe a little tomato or mushroom for topping. If it tastes good to you in the morning, why not eat it?

BROWN-BAG OR WHAT?
Of all the meals in a day, the one I least like preparing and eating is lunch. It seems such an unnecessary waste of time, unless you go out with friends. Sometimes we all get to do that, but for most of us, a good portion of our lunches are probably the brown-bag variety. So what can we do about lunches?

First, keep them simple—very simple. For yourself, a sandwich, fresh veggies and fruit, and something to drink. Or have a cup of yogurt, some fruit, and whole wheat crackers. Those of us who have sendentary jobs do not burn a lot of calories, so keep the intake down.

For the kids, I always found that a sandwich (vary the ingredients), a piece of fruit, and a couple of cookies seemed to be all they needed. They could buy milk, juice, or a soft drink at school. Teach them to make their own lunches just as soon as they are able. It's good training, it helps you, and it gives them a chance to be creative about what goes into the lunch.

Encourage your husband to help out with fixing lunches for everyone. If this is not his number one skill and you find you are making his lunch, watch the caloric intake. Men who sit at desks all day don't need a lot of calories any more than women do. And for all men—desk workers or laborers—watch the fat intake. Don't kill your husband with kindness in the form of high-fat foods.

A NEW IDEA

One recent study has determined that we would all be healthier if we ate about seventeen times a day. Now, I didn't say seventeen *meals* a day. The idea is that we graze—or forage—just taking the edge off our hunger and eating a wide range of food. It doesn't seem that our bodies were put together for three big meals a day.

This new idea may not be so new after all. It may be a holdover from the times when our ancestors roamed the fields and woods in search of food. They foraged for food. They'd eat a few berries from this bush, catch a rabbit and cook it, dig tubers from this area, and snack on nuts. They ate when they could find food, and when they couldn't they lived off the stored fat in their bodies.

Hermelin says, "People should either eat three small meals a day, supplemented by two 'power snacks,' as I call them, or five minimeals. Eating smaller meals throughout the day helps people think more clearly by keeping their blood sugar—the brain's major fuel—at a constant level. This also allows the overeater to eat fairly frequently and gives the undereater smaller, easier-to-digest portions."[2] Providing a nice steady flow of energy-producing calories to our bodies helps keep our metabolism up so that we are burning those calories rather than storing them as fat. I'm sure there will be more research on the subject, but if this is true, then our eating day should look something like this:

- Breakfast—as described above, keep it light
- Midmorning snack—easy-to-digest complex carbohydrates such as breads, cereals, fruits, and vegetables
- Light lunch—as described
- Midafternoon snack—same as midmorning or a container of yogurt
- Snack when arriving home from school or work—herb tea and whole wheat crackers, veggies, or fruit
- Light supper—ideas for this later in the chapter
- A couple of snacks spaced a couple of hours apart during the evening—juice, butter-free popcorn, a bagel, fruit bars
- A glass of milk at bedtime— calcium helps you sleep better

It's important to pay attention to what we are eating at those snacks. Watch the calories. (I used to dehydrate my own fruits and use them for snacks, until I realized all I'd removed was the water and not the calories. It

 would like to make my mother put a certain amount away every paycheck to insure her happy retirement.

—*Marcella*

was too easy to consume three bananas and half a pineapple in one sitting!) Watch the fat content. Eat lots of fruit and vegetables. Nutritionists say most of us are not getting enough servings of fruits and vegetables in a day.

One more thing to consider. The brain is about 75 percent fluid, and many office workers simply do not take in enough fluid in a day. Many times the "snack attack" you are feeling is actually your body's cry for water. We need sixty-four ounces (two quarts) of noncaffeinated fluid a day. Caffeine is a diuretic, so instead of adding fluid, it actually strips it from the body. (As I sit here writing this, I am experiencing a great deal of guilt because I'm a heavy coffee drinker who intends to drink more water and doesn't. I know I get the afternoon sags, and I'm wondering if it's all about water. Hmmm! Time to make a change.)

So take a pitcher or thermal jug of cool water and a glass and put them right in front of you on your desk. Drop in a slice of lemon or lime or a mint leaf for a little flavor. Of course, you can also replace fluids with fruit juice (this has calories), milk (this has calories), or caffeine-free diet soft drinks (have no calories, but take a look at the sodium content: sodium is salt, and you may end up thirstier than before). However you do it, get lots of fluids into your system. It may make you a more alert, productive worker.

INEVITABLY DINNER COMES ONCE A DAY

I rather suspect that for most of us dinner is the bugaboo of the day. It's the meal that we dread and wonder if we'll ever get through. It's the task that makes us want to give up and run away from home. We arrive home tired and irritable, and so does everyone else. Fixing dinner is not a pleasant prospect.

Rather than plunging right into the evening meal preparation, why not have a snack of crackers and juice (one of your seventeen minimeals) and a few minutes of rest before plunging into dinner preparation? Give the kids a snack, too. Just keep them from overeating, so their dinner won't be spoiled.

Now, let's see if we can figure out a plan and share some ideas about how to make this relentless task more manageable.

First of all, since so many of you said that you cook in bulk about once a week, let me recommend a book that might be a real help: *Once-a-Month Cooking* by Mimi Wilson and Mary Beth Lagerborg. These women have devised a cooking system that allows you to cook either once a month, twice a month, or once every two months. Included in the book is a low-fat bulk cooking plan. They suggest menus, tell you what to buy and when, what kind of containers you will need for cooking and freezing, and ideas for what to serve with the entree.[3]

One of the women who answered my survey has used the book. She said, "It has changed my life! I used to hate 4:30 every day because the kids were acting up and I had to make dinner and never knew what to make and never had all the ingredients for anything. This book shows you how to plan a month of meals, gives lists to shop from and a one-day cooking plan. Then you freeze everything. Now I don't dread dinnertime, and I can feed my husband and kids decent, tasty meals. It saves so much time—only one day of cooking, which I enjoy. And it saves dollars because

Make a list of your family's favorite meals and arrange them on a weekly basis. Everyone gets his favorite once a week. *—Sydna*

of fewer trips to the store and less buying of convenience foods. It has taken away a major stress factor in my day. I'm an organizer at heart, so I will be able to plan and freeze all my family's favorites and try new recipes while still only shopping for everything on one day and cooking on another day."

One of the things I like best about this plan is that on the day when you do the cooking—a massive all-day task—it's suggested you go out to eat. Isn't that a great idea?

If you can manage to take a day—probably for working women a Saturday—and fill your freezer with dinner-ready food, think of all the time you'll save later in the month. And why not get all the family members involved in the cooking? It would be great training. Children and husbands have a way of thinking that food magically appears on the table with little or nothing being done to make it happen, but it just isn't true. They need to learn there is some thought and labor behind the meals they eat.

The success of a bulk cooking day depends on organization. It takes planning, shopping ahead, proper storage containers, and enough freezer space.

A REVOLUTIONARY IDEA

I read about another truly unique dinner-making plan. It is a cooking co-op that four women started to provide meals for each other's families. Each woman cooks a meal for all four families once a week. On Fridays the families eat out. On Saturdays and Sundays they eat up the leftovers or individual family members cook for themselves, with husbands and children sometimes doing the cooking.

There are some real challenges to such a plan. The cook of the day has to have about three hours to prepare the meal. The families have to be willing to eat what's provided. There has to be open communication without offense — "That dish didn't reheat very well." There needs to be flexibility and support of others on the team. Severe dietary restrictions of a member of one of the families might create problems. Then, too, someone has to deliver the meals to the others' houses. That means participants need to live close to each other so that the deliveries can be made quickly.

It's an intriguing idea that would need some adaptation for working women. Working women would probably have to do the cooking on Saturday, freeze ahead, and deliver the frozen entree with the rest of the meal on the appointed day. But it's certainly another creative option to consider.

My Plan

My life has changed drastically in the last few years — empty nest, single again. But there was a time when I needed to have dinner on the table by 5:30 every night to get family members on their way to the second shift of their activities.

I was a working woman who got home about 4:45 in the afternoon. That meant I had to have everything thought out ahead of time. It meant that food had to be prepared and served quickly. There were severe dietary restrictions — no salt, no sugar, no fat—and I did not have a microwave at the time. Here's what I did:

First, I kept a menu file, organized by main meat ingredient (chicken recipes, beef recipes, etc.). There was also a division for no-meat dishes. On the same card as the entree there were suggestions for meal accompaniments—vegetables, breads, salads. If a recipe was needed, I wrote down the name of the cookbook and the page number so I didn't have to spend time looking for recipes. This was also a money saver, since it was easy to match recipes against the newspaper food specials of the week. If chicken was on special that week, I'd look in my file under chicken and see what kind of dish I could make.

Second, I made a menu-planning board by cutting business-sized envelopes in half to form pockets. I glued seven of these pockets to a poster board. I labeled them for each day of the week. Menu cards from the card file were then deposited in the pockets, and the chart hung on the side of the refrigerator. As the children grew older, they often referred to the cards to see what was planned for dinner. Often, they were able to start the meal.

As the children became teenagers and the level of their activities increased, our schedule seemed to be such that great changes could take place, and suddenly no one was coming to dinner. It wasn't any great crisis from a meal-planning standpoint. I simply pulled the cards from the pocket and moved them to another day of the week, or even to the next week, and was thankful one extra meal was planned.

We had a lot of drop-in company during those busy years. There were the children's friends, interns working in our church program, relatives, and others. I tried to keep a few prepared casseroles in the freezer for unexpected guests in case the planned dinner could not be expanded to include them.

ANOTHER IDEA

A long, long time ago I heard about an idea for cooking labeled DOLODOL. Each letter stood for a cooking plan for each day of the week:

> D — Double cooking (Sunday)
> O — One dinner only (Monday)
> L — Leftovers (Tuesday)
> O — One dinner only (Wednesday)
> D — Double cooking (Thursday)
> O — One dinner only (Friday)
> L — Leftovers (Saturday)

Well, I never could get the double cooking times to come out on a day when I had more time, but the concept was a good one. And I finally decided that when I did cook, I'd cook double and put half in the freezer. That could be used for a one-dinner night or even a leftover night or saved for unexpected company. One of my leftover nights was taken care of because I kept a stockpot and dropped bits and pieces of leftover meat, vegetables, and meat juices into it all week. Then for supper on Saturday evening I added lots of herbs and maybe some potatoes, rice, or barley to the stockpot and made a big kettle of soup. I bought a loaf of fresh French bread and made a green salad, and dinner was ready. A truly delicious leftover meal.

Another idea is to serve as much food as possible without cooking it. I did that a lot when family members' diets prohibited the use of salt, sugar, and fat, and I had no microwave. Raw carrots, broccoli, cauliflower, cabbage, and peas are better for you than the same vegetables are when cooked. Of course, they take less time to prepare, too.

Eat simply. Eliminate sauces and fancy preparation. Use a little margarine or olive oil, some herbs, and a little lemon juice to season vegetables that must be cooked. Once again, simple food is, in most cases, better for you.[4]

WHERE TO FIND COOKING IDEAS AND HELP

I'm not going to give you recipes in this book. There are dozens of cookbooks for fast cooking, and I've listed a few in the resources at the end of the chapter. Invest in one or two; teach your husband and kids some of the basic recipes from the cookbook; plan well, so husband and children know what's expected of them; and keep the necessary ingredients on hand.

Magazines are a constant source of recipes and ideas. Don't try them all—it's too time-consuming. But find a few good recipes, and use them again and again. Women's magazines often carry sections of recipes for fast-track cooking.

HOW TO BE A SMART GROCERY SHOPPER

When you wander into a grocery store, you are probably unaware that everything about that store and the placement of its goods has been designed to make you buy, buy, buy. Here are some insider tips:

- Store ads come out on Wednesday, so on Tuesdays displays are changed to move sale goods to a visible position.
- Usually sale items are in huge stacks at the ends of the aisles.
- Anything on sale will be at the best price it will be for at least a month. So buy lots of it if you need it.
- Sometimes stores are selling sale items at less than wholesale prices. They're called loss leaders and are used to attract customers. Loss leaders are usually staple items.
- Other specials can be found at eye level throughout the store. Staples will be on the bottom shelves.
- To save money, buy food that has had little preparation. Slicing, peeling, dicing, and packaging all have to be done by someone and all raise the price of the product.
- When a sale-priced product is sold out, always ask for a rain check. Ask for more than you think you'll need; you won't have to take them all if you don't want to, but if you only ask for three at the sale price and later decide you need

Along with my sister I am responsible for my grandparents, ages 92 and 103! I have to constantly ask God's intervention in reminding me there's a limit to what I can do. I have to ask him to help me with guilt. I have to say over and over, "It's OK if I tell them I can't be there every night." —Jan

four, you'll have to pay full price for the fourth.

- Buy store brands. They're manufactured by leading food processors. What you're not paying for is a lot of advertising. Savings on private labels can be as much as 70 percent over name-brand products.

- Try generic products, but remember that while a store's reputation rests on its store-brand label, generics are a different story. Some generic brands are not up to standard. But you're not risking much money to try a generic brand. If it's up to your standards, buy it.

- If saving money is important, beware of strategically placed displays containing high-priced items. They are put in your line of traffic on purpose to slow you down on your way to something you truly need.

- Be aware that store owners don't want it to be too easy for you to find items. They want you to look through lots of items before you find what you're looking for. They may even shift things around to keep you looking.

- Watch prices as they are scanned. All someone has to do is enter the wrong dollar amount for a scan code, and everyone who buys that product pays the wrong price until someone catches the error. Some stores have a policy stating that you receive the item free if you find an error.

- Watch for cross-merchandising. That's putting toys in the cereal aisle and salad dressing in the vegetable display case. It's convenient, but chances are the store has chosen its most expensive product for cross-merchandising.

- Stay out of the grocery store as much as possible. Every time you go—maybe just for a quart of milk—you'll come out with more than you intended to buy. I'm sure you know what I mean.

SUGGESTED READING

Jan Brink and Melinda Ramm, *S.N.A.C.K.S.: Speedy, Nutritious, and Cheap Kids' Snacks* (New York: New American Library, 1984).

Jill Burmeister, editor, *Complete Quick and Easy Cookbook* (Des Moines, Iowa: Meredith Corporation, 1983).

The Busy Cook's Cookbook (Pleasantville, N.Y.: Reader's Digest Association, 1993).

Pasquale Carpino, *Pasquale's Kitchen Express Cookbook* (Indianapolis: Kimberly, 1990).

Irena Chalmers, *The Working Family's Cookbook* (New York: Barron, 1993).

Jean Hewitt, *Family Circle Quick Menu Cookbook* (New York: Times Books, 1978).

Madhur Jaffrey, *Madhur Jaffrey's Cookbook: Easy East/West Menus* (New York: Harper and Row, 1989).

Ruth Ann Manners and William Manners, *The Quick and Easy Vegetarian Cookbook* (New York: M. Evans, 1978).

Robyn Supraner, *Quick and Easy Cookbook,* (Mahwah, N.J.: Troll Assoc., 1981).

Weight Watchers Quick and Easy Menus (New York: NAL-Dutton, 1989).

Mimi Wilson and Mary Beth Lagerborg, *Once-a-Month Cooking* (Colorado Springs: Focus on the Family, 1992).

PART
THREE

*Thriving
at the Office*

CHAPTER 8

Finding the Perfect Job

L ike finding the love of your life, finding the perfect job is a combination of being at the right place at the right time; being mature enough to recognize the opportunity; having the ability to know if your skills, personality, and temperament are right for this match; and being able to evaluate if this is something you want to commit to.

The truth is that when you find the job of your life, you'll be spending more of your waking hours with it and the people there than you will with the love of your life. So it's important to be careful, to think through the implications of taking a job, and to take enough time to find the right job.

Once you've started a job, it can be tough to move up within the company. You get locked in very quickly to a system and a job description. Secretaries are perceived as secretaries, and it is difficult for them to move to a management position even if their training, experience, and skills warrant the promotion.

So where do you begin? How can you be sure you're taking a job that has a future? You begin at the beginning

*D*on't be afraid to experiment. Be willing to start with something menial that has potential for great growth.   —*Janet*

with a good self-evaluation of your strengths and weaknesses, and you begin with a great resume.

BEGIN AT THE BEGINNING

There is no way you can know what kind of job you should be looking for without first having a clear picture of who you are and of your strengths and weaknesses. This evaluation must be an honest, positive assessment of skills, interests, talents, and training. Without it, it is impossible to write or speak to a prospective employer with confidence. On the other side of the equation, one of our greatest strengths is to know our weaknesses—to admit them and to either find ways to compensate for them or find a job where those weaknesses are not a problem.

I'll never forget when Sandra burst into my office for her job interview. She dripped confidence. She knew her strengths and weaknesses. She knew what she wanted from life. You could feel it. You could see it in the way she carried herself. You could hear it in her words. And she got the job—a sales/marketing position.

But how do we identify our weaknesses and our strengths? In this chapter and the next are some ideas and measuring devices for determining strengths and weaknesses. Career counseling can also be a very valuable tool if you can afford it. It is particularly helpful if you come from a dysfunctional job situation. (Employment situations can be as dysfunctional as families and exhibit many of the same characteristics.)

In preparing to write this chapter I pulled out a folder of materials I had used for self-evaluation when job hunting. I had put together a job profile—a job description of what I thought would be an ideal job, a couple of ideal locations for that job, a time frame in which I hoped the new job would happen, a style of working that would be ideal, and an acceptable salary level. As I read through it, I was shocked, because the job I now have is the exact duplication, in terms of job description, salary, and location, of what I wrote down on paper eleven months before the position was offered to me. I can't promise you the same results, but I now understand that knowing what I wanted to do with my life guided me toward this time and this place.

Before I worked through the process of creating a career evaluation, I was confused, unclear about who I was or where I wanted to go, and driving everyone around me crazy. Someone called me unfocused. That might have been an understatement. A good portion of my frustration came from the fact that I had walked away from a job I loved, because the company was in serious decline. It had truly become dysfunctional and was eating away at my insides.

I really loved that line of work—management and editing—and had no desire to give it up. That became apparent as I worked through the self-evaluation. Because there were no opportunities for me in that locale, the next step was clear. I had to relocate. As soon as I decided to relocate, I opened the door to more job opportunities. I realize not everyone can pull up stakes and start over some other place, but if you can, you will increase the possibilities of finding the perfect job. If you can't relocate, you might be able to take some courses, upgrade skills, learn something entirely new and in that way find a better, more challenging job.

I've come back to what I love doing best — writing, editing, managing a team with a growing organization in an area of the country that is not only beautiful but offers several career possibilities besides the one I'm in. I feel the salary I am earning is commensurate with my level of responsibility and experience.

Many women are thrown back into the workforce after being in the home for many years. Divorce, a husband's illness or death, or a downturn in family finances for some other reason often catapults women into a job. It's tough, especially if the circumstances don't allow time for re-training.

If there is even a little time, it would be best to work with an employment agency (even state agencies can be helpful). They will give a battery of tests to determine where a reentering woman might best fit into the workplace. If you hate sitting at a desk for eight hours a day, maybe the best job for you would be in a bakery. If you can't be on your feet all day long, you probably won't be able to be a cashier at a supermarket.

Many reentering women underestimate their skills and the experience they've gained in running a household. I did. I didn't realize that handling the household money, training children, settling disputes, coping with crises, and coordinating complex schedules of family members were all training me to be a good manager.

When I went back to work, it was as an associate editor. I never dreamed that two years later I would be asked to manage the department and multiple publications. I didn't think I could accept the responsibility, but I decided to try—and I discovered I'd learned a lot all those years I'd been a homemaker.

It could be that a reentering woman will need some training or upgrading of skills. If a woman has had no computer training, for instance, it would be wise to take some classes, since so much of our lives today is tied to computers. Beside computers, work situations are filled with electronic equipment such as modems, sorters, fax machines, complicated copy machines, security devices, pagers, high-tech telephone systems, and a host of others. It would be wise to learn what these machines are for and how to use them. And even if you've decided to go to work packing fruit in a warehouse, don't think you can escape knowing something about some of these pieces of equipment.

AN IDEA FOR SELF-EVALUATION

Check the business/career section of your public library or local bookstore for self-evaluation information. There are lots of books available because this is an area of great concern to many working people. (A few good ones are listed at the end of this chapter.)

Here, though, is a simple idea that helped me. Make a chart with three columns. Label the first column My Needs—in my career, this is what's important to me to be, feel, try.

Under this column write down all the things that you value in a job. For example, my chart (prepared before I wrote the career profile I mentioned earlier) listed these things:

- To exhibit leadership
- To encourage others by giving them opportunities
- To make a positive contribution
- To solve problems and leave the system better than I found it
- To earn what I'm worth
- To be happy in my work and feel good about myself

Label column two Ways My Current Job Meets/Doesn't Meet My Needs. It was when I made this list that I began to see that my present situation was not helping me and that I was not happy. At the time, I was freelancing—working alone out of my home—and trying to start a newsletter. My list read:

- Leadership—I have no one to lead
- Positive contribution—Not until I get the newsletter started
- Problems to solve—I have plenty of these, but I also create them for myself
- Earning what I'm worth—Making almost nothing
- To be happy in my work—I'm not happy

It didn't take me long to see that I had to make some changes. I had to find meaningful work. I had to stop trying to do something I didn't know how to do.

Label the third column Opportunities. Here, start to list

ideas for dealing with the problems listed in column two. When I got to this step, it quickly became apparent that I was not cut out to work in isolation and that I would probably never be happy freelancing.[1]

This evaluation process was followed by another one in which I listed:

- Personal priorities
- Interests
- Skill areas
- Preferred work style
- Knowledge and experience

I then tried to visualize the perfect job—what I'd be doing, who I'd be working with, what kind of office setting I'd have—and always underneath it all were the desires to encourage others, give helpful information, make a product that was meaningful and had far-reaching influence. Because I am a visual/kinesthetic/analytical learner, it helped me to put this information on a chart, too, so I could see all of it at the same time and analyze it.

WRITING A RESUME

Once you've completed your self-evaluation, writing a resume for those jobs that require it becomes a much simpler task. There are dozens of books about how to write the perfect resume. Get a couple of them and learn how the experts do it.

As an employer who's looked at

Investigate, learn about the area you're interested in. Volunteer, if that's applicable.

—Eugenie

hundreds of resumes, let me tell you some of the things that impress me:

- *Professional-looking resume on a good grade of paper.* When an employer is looking through stacks of resumes, it's easy to be influenced by a visually pleasing, easy-to-read resume. If you don't have desktop capabilities on your computer — or maybe you don't have a computer — have someone do a high-quality laser print for you.

- *Short and well-organized resume (one or two pages).* An employer is not interested in reading your life's history on a resume. Just a simple listing of your experience is sufficient.

- *Skills, achievements, interests listed in a succinct, easy-to-read manner.* As an employer, I know what I need in terms of skills for a certain position. I don't want to, and won't, search through your resume to find them.

- *Something that tells me you have vision, goals, and a desire to move forward in your career.* I'm often looking for raw talent, a teachable attitude. I want to hire someone who's eager to join the team and learn the job.

- *Something that tells me you have transferable skills.* Rarely does an applicant fit a job description 100 percent. But certain skills will transfer to other kinds of work very nicely.

- *A confidence that says you believe in yourself.* For that reason, it's sometimes best to put together a resume that doesn't just list achievements and training but that shows a broader scope of projects you've worked on, the results, and what you learned from the process. Here's an example: "In 1987 I devised a plan to cut our manufacturing costs on a certain product by 30 percent. Revenue in our division increased in that calendar year by 15 percent as a direct result of the implementation of the concept. In working out that idea, I learned how to analyze an existing work plan; formulate a new and better economic model; and implement the plan by choosing key workers, overseeing the operation in its beginning stages, and turning the operation over to a trained worker when the right time came. I believe the knowledge gained will be transferable to other work situations where analysis and implementation are needed."

NETWORKING AS A WAY OF FINDING A JOB

Possibly no factor is more important to finding a job than networking. As soon as your objectives about the job you are seeking are clear, and as soon as you truly know what you have to offer, you can begin to let friends and acquaintances know you are looking for a job. The more people who know, the more opportunities you will have to find the right job. Friends know us well and are often able to identify those employment opportunities that fit us best.

There are several kinds of networking. There's the informal variety, just described, in which we simply let friends and family know we are looking. This informal networking can also include friends in the industry of our choice. They

*I*nterview your prospective boss for the role of "employer" in your life. Be gracious, of course. —*Vinnie*

are the ones who have their ear to the rail and know when a job will open.

The other kind of networking is more formal, in which we ask for an interview with a company, perhaps even if there is no opening at the time. The purpose is to gather information about the industry or field of interest, to let key people in the industry know we are job hunting, and to get contact names of other employers. Eventually you will find someone who needs an employee with your skills.

The key question to ask in formal networking interviews is, Since you are not in need of an employee with my skills at this particular time, do you know other companies that might be looking? And a follow-up question of great importance is, And who should I try to contact there? Get the name of someone inside that other company if at all possible.

It's good to follow up this meeting with a thank-you note. The more times a person sees your name, the more likely he is to remember it. He may not have an opening now, but in business and industry things can change rapidly from day to day. Besides, it's just plain nice to send a note.

APPLYING FOR THAT SPECIAL JOB

After the self-evaluation, after the resume writing, after networking and making the contacts, after filling out the application forms and doing the pretesting, finally you come to I-day—interview day. There's no way to avoid it.

It can be scary because you are being evaluated as you sit in a future employer's office, answering all kinds of questions.

I recently helped my boss interview candidates for a secretarial position. I could see the strain on the candidates, but just for the record, there's a tremendous amount of strain on the employer, too. It's crucial that we bring the right person into the position. It has to be someone who has the necessary skills and relates well to all the staff—office mix is very important.

It's interesting to be with a candidate who is focused, who knows what she wants, who is determined, who'll work through the process with patience. That candidate stands head and shoulders above her competition.

From my experience, expensive tailored suits, leather handbags, and fancy shoes are not important, but neatness, appropriateness of dress, voice, poise, and body language are all vitally important. One of the main purposes of a personal interview is to find out how this person responds to stressful situations, how she will present herself to the clientele, and if her telephone voice and demeanor are pleasant.

WORK AT FINDING A JOB

Yesterday I talked with a man who has recently decided to leave the ministry and enter the business world. I asked what he is doing these days. His reply was that he is working full-time at finding the right position. This is a major career shift for him, and he wants to do it right.

Therein lies a secret for anyone looking for work or trying to relocate to a better-paying or more satisfying job.

Work at it full-time. Work at it like a job. If you are unemployed, you are employed—you are in the business of finding new work. And you will find it exhausting work at that.

This man had rented a little office and set up a phone, a fax, and a desk. He goes there every morning and works until quitting time.

Most of us would not be able to rent an office, but we could set up a little workplace at home. The key is to find contacts, send letters, make calls, and follow up on interviews. Eventually, it will pay off.

If you are willing to move laterally and take a job at the same wage you've been making, it will be easier to find a job than if you are trying to move up. If you are in one of the helping or service industries, it may be easier to find work than if you are seeking a management position. Secretaries, laborers, domestics, service people, and entry-level workers find it fairly easy to get a job or to relocate. There aren't enough of these helping-profession people. Particularly there aren't enough who truly care about their work. They are in great demand.

If you are moving at a managerial or executive level, it's going to take longer to relocate. In fact, many people seeking management positions despair of ever finding the right job, and they begin to think about getting a job delivering newspapers. There is a great deal of downsizing of companies these days, and it tends to hit middle management the hardest.

Don't despair. Hang in there. This comes from one who despaired, who threatened not to hang in there. But in the end God came on the scene and did what I couldn't do and placed me in the job of my first choice. Remember, God is interested in you and your well-being, and he's for you. Sometimes we come to the place where we just have to throw our whole weight on him. You can find the job of your life. But it may take some concentration on your part, it may take some retraining, and it's pretty certain to take some time. But it is doable. So, if you're job hunting, be encouraged—things are looking up.

SUGGESTED READING

Stephen R. Covey, *The Seven Habits of Highly Effective People* (New York: Simon and Schuster, 1989).

Cathie Cowie and Rhonda Kline, *Selling You.* A book that walks you through the self-evaluation, the preparation, and the whole process of finding a new job. Order the book from Cathie Cowie and Rhonda Kline (human resource consultants), Alston Kline, Inc., 320 Dayton St., Suite 125, Edmonds, WA 98020, phone 206-843-1458.

Robert P. Downe, *The Better Book for Getting Hired: How to Write a Great Resume, Sell Yourself in the Interview, and Get That Job* (Vancouver: International Self-Counsel, 1992).

Richard Earle and David Imrie, *Your Vitality Quotient: The Clinically Proven Program That Can Reduce Your Body Age and Increase Your Zest for Life* (New York: Warner, 1990).

Warren S. Feld, *How High Can You Fly: The Ultimate Career and Resume Guide for the Upwardly Mobile Professional* (New York: Prentice Hall, 1986).

Loretta D. Foxman, *Resumes That Work: How to Sell Yourself on Paper* (New York: Wiley, 1992).

Charles Good, *Resumes for Re-Entry: A Handbook for Women* (Manassas, Va.: Impact, 1993).

Katharine Hansen, *Dynamic Cover Letters* (Berkeley, Calif.: Ten Speed, 1990).

Herman Holtz, *Beyond the Resume: How to Land the Job You Want* (New York: Bennu, 1985).

Working Woman magazine is a monthly compendium of helpful information. Although it is feminist in perspective, many articles are valuable, and you can read about how to find the right job.

CHAPTER 9

Don't Just Hang in There!

I've been rereading Marsha Sinetar's wonderful book *Do What You Love, the Money Will Follow.* The book is about how not to "just hang in there." It's about getting a job that has meaning and one that challenges your full potential.

She begins her book with these words:

> About ten years ago, I began to experience a great longing to change my life. The thought of letting go of what I had—a well-paying, secure job; a beautiful home; friends and family nearby—was truly terrifying. I who had always clung to outward forms of security, I who had wanted guarantees in every part of my life, also ignored the inner dissatisfactions and urgings I felt.
>
> Years before, this prompting from within had started. And I had ignored it. I distracted myself with a respected career and with the inevitable promotions that came my way. I distracted myself even more successfully with an accumulation of material rewards and symbols of success. The unknown was too fright-

I **am an adult child of an alcoholic (ACOA) and said I'd never work with alcoholics. But here I am, a supervisor of a drug and alcohol facility. It's important to be open to God's leading.** —*Joyce*

ening to me. This, despite the fact that by all outward appearances I was a creative, spontaneous and enthusiastic person.

In reality, I did not truly trust myself. I was afraid to cross uncharted, unconventional waters to get to a more desirable place in life, afraid that—when truth be told—I would not have the requisite strength and competence to accomplish what I so dearly wanted. I could not even imagine how to start. While I did believe the adage "What man can conceive, he can achieve," I couldn't conceive of doing what I knew I would love. My mind clung so desperately to the familiar.[1]

Does any of this sound familiar? Could it be that you too are struggling with the need to make changes in your working life and you can't even begin to imagine how to start making the needed changes?

It's important to know that you don't have to just hang in there. You can find work that fits you, that is meaningful to you. It may not be a job in which you climb the corporate ladder. It may not be the job you or someone else, at one time, thought you should pursue. In fact, you may leave the lofty halls of corporate business to begin a business that in some people's eyes may seem very humble. There have been those who have left corporate jobs to establish cleaning businesses, picture-framing shops, or child-care facilities and have found more meaning in their lives than ever before. Some have moved to smaller companies and have found the casual, more intimate work environment just right for them. Changing your work situation is frightening at any stage in life, and it is especially scary to midlife women. But it is possible to make a positive change. Knowing yourself will help you move in the right direction.

STEPPING UP

It's often difficult for a worker to change roles within a company. We are very quickly pegged to a certain job and skill level. Even if a worker is overqualified for a position, once she is in a role, it's tough to get out. In fact, sometimes it seems the only way to make a change is to change companies.

Jennifer, a successful editor, decided to make a major shift in her life and move across the country. Because it was essential that she find work immediately upon arriving at her new destination, she took a job that was below her qualifications.

After a few months in that mismatched position—that of production coordinator—she changed jobs and became a print buyer. The position was only marginally better for her, and she was still not using her talents of writing and editing. She was underchallenged and complained to the human resources department about the problem. She even suggested some areas she might develop for the company, but all to no avail. She wanted to be an editor, but she was not seen in that role. Because this company did not respond to her needs, she eventually chose to take a job with another company as communications director.

Those who want to advance within a company are probably going to have to succeed at the projects they are given, challenge the system, ask questions, get training, and/or change departments. In some companies there are other ways to get ahead, but they are not options for Christian women. It's well known that power struggles, keeping the rules, fraternizing with the right people, sleeping with the boss, and other forms of manipulation and exploitation are used to get advancement. What a hollow victory it must be to know you have been advanced not because you have superior skills or insight but because you've played up to the right people in the prescribed way!

IS THERE A GLASS CEILING?

I don't think there's any question about it. There is a glass ceiling. There is a level to which women can rise easily. After that, advancement, while not impossible, becomes very difficult.

Officially, the glass ceiling is that invisible barrier that separates men and women when it comes to attaining top positions in *Fortune* 500 firms.[2] On a less lofty level, it's the barrier that keeps any woman from being advanced simply because she is a woman. This happens in all kinds of companies and in Christian ministries as well.

A woman limited by a glass ceiling has two options: break through it or leave the company. Many women simply walk away, take their skills with them, and start new businesses. And many of those new businesses are thriving. Women entrepreneurs make up one of the strongest, most rapidly growing segments of the business world. If a woman decides to stay in her company and shatter the glass ceiling, she's got to remember there are likely to be a lot of shards flying about for a while.

I have a friend who decided to challenge her particular system and finally won. She became a vice president with her own line of product. It wasn't easy. She had to try harder than the men in the company until she proved she could be a valuable profit center. The price she's had to pay is that some people, viewing her only from the outside, think she's tough and aggressive. To some extent, it's true. While on one side she's a tender, compassionate mother and wife, on the other side—the business side—she's had to learn to stand up for her own rights. It's taken a lot of courage on her part and a lot of not listening to the criticism.

Perhaps even more subtle than the company glass ceiling is the glass ceiling within many of us. Our own attitude says, "I'm a woman. I'll never be considered for a promotion because I am. And if I ever got the position, I would be treated differently than a man. I might not even get the same salary as a male counterpart."

Unfortunately, much of it is true. But we defeat ourselves by continuing to have an attitude and a perception of ourselves that relegates us to an inferior position. We have to remember that we are created in God's image. When God created man and woman, he created them both in his own image, both with worth and value.

I've thought a lot about the Scripture that speaks of men and women as fellow heirs of grace (1 Peter 3:7). If we are fellow heirs, we stand side by side, equal in God's eyes.

While men and women naturally have differing abilities in some areas, there is nothing that inherently makes one gender more talented, creative, or intelligent than the other. Many of our differences are cultural and learned.

A coworker of mine has an interesting flip-flop in his marriage. His wife loves to build fences, put in lawns, and hang drywall. Larry, on the other hand, is more given to sit-down projects—writing, editing, reading. They have worked it out beautifully between them.

Their son, however, made an interesting observation. He told his dad he didn't think he wanted to do "women's work." By that he meant doing the physical kinds of projects his mother does. He's more like his dad and prefers the quieter pursuits.

Our culture says women should fulfill one kind of role and men another. I know I'm affected by this, because when I meet a male nurse or a male secretary, I'm still surprised.

Sometimes I truly wonder what God had in mind when he created us male and female. What were the roles he intended for us to fulfill? What would this world be like in terms of relationships if there had never been a fall from grace? Reading about Jesus Christ, I know he values womanhood. I know he is grieved when a woman is discriminated against because of her gender.

Personally, I believe that if the church had, through the centuries, championed the rights of women instead of being one of the worst offenders against them, there would have been no need for a feminist movement. There would be no strident, militant women trying to prove themselves. There would be fewer abortions. There would have been more progress in society as women's creativity and insights were released and given full expression.

GETTING THE TRAINING YOU NEED

We are living in a day of adult education. Almost every city of any size offers evening classes for adults. You can take classes from the most basic subjects clear through to a master's program by enrolling for one or two classes at a time and continuing to plug away until the degree is earned.

A number of my work colleagues are in various stages of degree programs. I watch them hurry around late in the afternoon, trying to get everything finished so they can whisk off to class. It's tough. But these people, men and women, know what they want from life, and they are going after it.

So how do we start getting the training we need? Here's how:

- Know what you want and where you are headed.
- Pick up a class schedule from your local university, college, or community college.
- Talk with an academic advisor and devise a plan of action.
- Register, pay the fees, and get started.

*D*etermine what you'd really like to do, where you'd like to work, and go for it. —*Nan*

It may sound like I'm oversimplifying, but the old adage says, "A journey of a thousand miles begins with a single step." The place to begin is here and now. Pick up the catalog, pick up the phone, get motivated, get moving.

There are other options besides going back to school. Specialized seminars abound. While they are expensive, it is a place to learn specific information in a concentrated way and in a hurry.

A self-prescribed course of reading may be another way to acquire the knowledge you need to get ahead. Such a reading program can be tailored to your lifestyle and fit in around other existing demands. While you will not have a diploma to hand an employer, you will have up-to-date skills and knowledge that will further your career and make you valuable.

THRIVING ON CHANGE

One of the surest things in life is change. No matter what your job may be, no matter what your home situation, no matter how constant you want your life to be, change will happen. We can't stop it, we can't hold it back. Change only stops when we are dead. So take heart: if life is changing, then life is happening. You're still alive. And it may be that the more change there is, the more life is happening for you.

Years ago my brothers and I got our families together. We had all these wonderful little kids running around and playing together. It was a happy time, and we enjoyed it, though we probably didn't treasure it as much as we should have. Now the kids have grown up, are getting married, and are moving in many different directions. While we'd like to recapture what we had, we can't. The river of time has moved along, and we can't go back to what we had. That's not bad. We have something new and wonderful.

Some of these now-grown-up kids will soon have kids of their own, who will bring freshness and new life into the family.

I use that illustration because most of us can relate to it. We sometimes want time to stand still, but it doesn't. We sometimes want to avoid change, but we can't. Change will happen. We can either embrace it with great joy or fight it and make ourselves (and everyone around us) miserable.

As far as our jobs go, think about the last fifteen or twenty years. Think about the innovations in technology that have taken place. Computers have changed the world forever. Facsimile machines have increased the speed of business transactions to a breakneck pace. Cellular phones and all related technology have made the world accessible to us no matter where we are—land, sky, sea.

In addition, knowledge keeps doubling every few years. Take any field of knowledge and try to keep up with the advances in it. It matters not if it's the computer industry, the clothing business, or the food industry. It's almost impossible to keep up. Multiply those areas by hundreds, and you can see why many of us are on information overload.

HOW DO WE COPE WITH CHANGE?

First of all, we cope with change by accepting that it will happen. By just accepting the fact, we begin to diffuse it. Change will happen to you, your family, your body. Change will happen in your company. If the company is healthy, much of the change will relate to growth. If the company is dying, the change will relate to a slow death. Believe me, the former is much more fun, although it is also more challenging. The systems and rules that worked yesterday

Larry Burkett of Christian Financial Concepts has an assessment to help people choose a job that is right for their talents, financial needs, and family situations. There are several tests such as Harrison-O'Shea and Myers-Briggs Inventories that can also be helpful.

—Cathy

in such a company do not work today. It takes creative, flexible people to keep up with a rapidly growing company.

Second, you can better accept change if you are prepared or are preparing for it. Much change related to business has to do with new techniques, new ideas, new ways of doing things. Keeping up with change by taking classes, attending seminars, or reading in the field helps you be ready for and maybe even ahead of the changes.

Third, try to be a part of the decision making related to the changes happening in your company. Realize that your input is vital and worthy of being heard. Help to shape the change if you can. Unfortunately, decisions are often made without the advice and consideration of the people they will affect. Workers are often left out of the loop of decision making.

Fourth, if you cannot go along with the change, and if you've talked with your superiors and found the system is set, then you will have to change jobs. Sometimes for ethical or educational reasons we cannot make the changes demanded by a company. And sometimes the change taking place has nothing to do with educational or ethical issues; it is just too uncomfortable for us. In such situations we have to leave and find something else to do. Since changing jobs is a traumatic event, it is something we'd all rather avoid, but you cannot sacrifice your well-being on the altar of your employment.

WHEN IT'S TIME TO MOVE ON

When the time comes to move on to another job, it needs to be done quickly and with as much consideration for others as possible. When you've landed another job, or even if you haven't but you need to go, it's important to wrap up those tasks that depend on information you carry in your head. Somewhere down the line, it will be very satisfying for you to know you did all you could to leave the job in good condition.

Leave quickly once the announcement has been made. I once watched a woman who had considerable responsibility in a company resign and walk away from the job in a little over a week. I thought, *How can she do that? She'll leave behind such a hole that it will put the company in a terrible predicament.* When I asked her about it, she said, "Gwen, it's the best way. There's nothing worse than staying too long." The hole she left resembled that made by pulling your hand out of a pail of water. Although she had been a valuable, contributing employee while she worked there, within days the company moved on without her.

Another woman in the same company resigned but stayed on to help out until the company replaced her. The company moved on without her too—even though she was still around. Decisions were made, and she was not included because she was not going to be there. Her opinions and ideas suddenly bore no weight at all. She ended up staying several months beyond her resignation, and it was devastating to her emotionally.

When my turn came to leave, I'd learned from these two examples. I resigned and left within two weeks. I only stayed that long because I was in a key position and other key people were on vacation. Leaving quickly was best for me and for them.

Another point about leaving a company: Empty threats—noises about resigning—that may or may not be serious can be taken as a signal of discontent by your employer. He or she just may take you up on it. Don't resign if you're not resigning, or the next thing you know you may not have a job.

It happens more often than you might think. I've had three employees resign but not really mean it, and all of them found themselves without work. The first one resigned but hoped we'd beg her to stay. Actually, the company was looking for an excuse to let her go. The second resigned then wanted to come back and thought we owed her the job. We didn't; we'd hired someone else to take her place. The third resigned and then decided she wished she hadn't and took her case to a judge. She lost her case, because once you resign, you've resigned.

So think it through before you jump off the ship. The water out there may be deeper and colder than you thought possible. Maybe it's better to work with the crew to help fix the ship.

STRETCH!

I once read that changing jobs can add as much as five years to your life. I don't know what kind of research has been done to corroborate that statement, but I do know, from personal experience, that a new job can give you a new lease on life, especially if it is challenging.

Finding a new job is exciting and terrifying all at once. Many of us fear failure and so take the safe jobs, the ones we are sure we can do, and because of that decision, we miss the thrill and excitement of the stretch. A job that is just like the one you left is no challenge.

Of course, finding a job that is too difficult can be devastating. The key is to find one for which you are qualified but which still has enough stretch in it to keep you challenged.

Once again, knowing your skills, having evaluated them from the standpoint of honesty, neither underestimating nor overestimating them, is one of the most valuable assets in finding the right job.

Most of my life I've taken jobs that were just a little too hard for me. It's given me the feeling of being in water up to my eyes. I have to tip my head back and keep looking up to keep my nose above water for a while. Then one day I realize I've grown enough so that the water is below my nose.

Growth can happen to you, too. So don't be afraid to stretch when reaching for a new job.

SUGGESTED READING

Richard Nelson Bolles, *How to Create a Picture of Your Ideal Job or Next Career* (Berkeley, Calif.: Ten Speed, 1989).

Charlene Canape, *The Part-Time Solution: The New Strategy for*

Managing Your Career While Managing Motherhood (New York: Harper and Row, 1990).

Stephen R. Covey, *The Seven Habits of Highly Effective People* (New York: Simon and Schuster, 1989).

Andrew DuBrin, *Your Own Worst Enemy: How to Overcome Career Self-Sabotage* (New York: AMACOM, 1992).

Lee Ellis and Larry Burkett, *Your Career in Changing Times* (Chicago: Moody Press, 1993).

Julianne Fowler, *How to Get the Job You Want in Tough Times* (Los Angeles: Lowell House, 1991).

George B. Graen, *Unwritten Rules for Your Career: The Fifteen Secrets for Fast-Track Success* (New York: Wiley, 1989).

James Gray, *The Winning Image: Present Yourself with Confidence and Style for Career Success* (New York: AMACOM, 1993).

Betsy Jaffe, *Altered Ambitions: What's Next in Your Life?* (New York: Donald I. Fine, 1991).

George L. Morrisey, *Creating Your Future: Personal Strategic Planning for Professionals* (San Francisco: Berrett-Koehler, 1992).

Laura Pedersen, *Street-Smart Career Guide: A Step-by-Step Guide to Your Career Development* (New York: Crown, 1993).

Wilbur L. Perry, *The Fast Track to Success: Easy Ways to Become More Successful in Achieving Your Career and Money Goals* (Englewood Cliffs, N. J.: Prentice-Hall, 1982).

Carl D. Peterson, *Staying in Demand: How to Make Job Offers Come to You* (New York: McGraw-Hill, 1993).

Marsha Sinetar, *Do What You Love, the Money Will Follow: Discovering Your Right Livelihood* (New York: Dell, 1989).

Janice Weinberg, *How to Win the Job You Really Want* (New York: Holt, 1989).

Neil M. Yeager, *Careermap: Deciding What You Want, Getting It, and Keeping It* (New York: Wiley, 1988).

Baila Zeitz, *The Best Companies for Women* (New York: Simon and Schuster, 1988).

CHAPTER 10

Handling Tough Job Situations

Ever since Anita Hill blazed onto the front pages of our newspapers and into our living rooms on marathon telecasting with her charges of sexual harassment against Clarence Thomas, and ever since the infamous Tailhook scandal, we've been looking at office relationships in a new light.

Not only are we looking at sexual harassment, but at discrimination, response to authority, work jealousy, manipulation, dishonesty of employer or employee, and many more tough situations.

SEXUAL HARASSMENT

Just what is sexual harassment? Most women and many employers are confused about what truly constitutes sexual harassment. It ranges from making sexual innuendoes to a man's putting his hand down a woman's blouse. It can include compliments about a woman's legs, a request to go out for drinks after work, a suggestion that if she'd cooperate he could make things go better for her at work. In a mild form it's pestering a person with sexual implications. In an extreme form it's being thrown up against the wall of a hotel

hen something goes wrong with workplace relationships, I speak my mind in a just and even-toned way.

—Karen

hallway and being fondled, which is what happened in the Tailhook scandal. And we can't overlook the fact that men are also being harassed by their female employers.

One writer says, "The most common behavioral definition of sexual harassment is 'Deliberate and/or repeated sexual or sex-based behavior that is not welcome, not asked for, and not returned.'"[1] Sexual harassment happens at all levels of employment. Waitresses and secretaries have been putting up with it for years. Surveys report that women who are high up in corporations are frequently harassed. Also, women working in male-dominated organizations are harassed more than those in more equal environments. And that survey also reports that 60 percent of respondents said they either had been personally harassed or knew someone who had. This information is based only on *reported* cases of harassment; evidence indicates that most sexual harassment goes unreported.

WOMEN ARE NOT TO BLAME

It's not the way a woman dresses or behaves that causes sexual harassment. It's not her sensitivity to off-color jokes. It's not even about office romances that have gone sour.

Sexual harassment in most cases is probably not even about sex. It's more likely about power and control. It's about intimidation. It's about climbing to the top of the corporate ladder. It's about who's in charge here. When perpetrated against women, it's sometimes an attempt to remind them to keep their place—that place being defined by old cultural patterns, men's fears, and an archaic business and economic structure.

Those who are harassed are the young, and they are preyed on by the old. The powerful prey on the less powerful. In 83 percent of the cases, the harasser is in a more powerful position than the one being harassed.

Women consider sexual harassment on the job a problem of major significance, ranking right up there with salary inequities, inadequate child care and elder care, and prejudice against promoting women.[2]

WHAT TO DO IF IT HAPPENS TO YOU

Most of us, when harassed, try to pretend that it didn't happen. We hope that if we ignore it, the problem will go away. It usually doesn't! We must not underestimate the damage done by sexual harassment. It is devastating to a woman's self-esteem, making her feel like a piece of meat rather than a valued employee. It can cause all kinds of stress-related illnesses, such as chronic fatigue, headaches, sleeplessness, heart palpitations, colds, and even urinary tract infections.

Sexual harassment cannot be allowed to continue, first of all because it is wrong. Also, it is devastating to the woman who is involved, as well as being detrimental to the perpetrator and to the morale of the other workers.

First of all, try to prevent sexual harassment by saying no loudly and clearly. There can be no waffling, no teasing. Say no and mean it. Let the perpetrator know that if it happens again you will turn him in to the human resources department.

Of course, the problem may be complicated by the fact that the harasser is the boss; there is no human resources department; there's nowhere to turn him in; your job is on the line, and you need your job. If you are being sexually harassed and if there doesn't seem to be any way to deal with it, at least document the problem. Write down or make a tape recording of what happened and when. Record conversations accurately—do it the same day of the incident so that your memory is fresh. Even if you do nothing with the accumulated documentation, it will give you a sense of taking control of the situation. And if you end up taking the case to the authorities, such documentation will be looked on favorably by the courts.

If you have been sexually harassed and decide to fight back, be warned that your particular workplace may not have caught up to life in the real world. Your company may not be aware of the seriousness of charges of sexual harassment. There may be no other way for you to get the company's attention than by suing.

There is a lot of information available about this subject. If you think sexual harassment is going on in your workplace, read the information that is available and speak with your supervisor about the problem. If he refuses to act, then it's time to consult with your human resources department. Ask for training on this subject for both men and women. Above all, keep trying to work through it.

WORKPLACE JEALOUSIES AND COMPLAINING
It happens for all kinds of reasons. Someone gets jealous

because she has been passed over for a raise. A single parent is jealous because a coworker is in a two-income situation and has more spendable income than she does. Another worker is jealous because she's not called into conference meetings with the boss.

Jealousies occur even over such seemingly mundane things as who gets a window in the office or a bigger desk or higher partitions around her workstation. The opportunities for jealousies are many.

Nothing undermines the morale of a staff any more quickly than whining brought on by real or perceived inequities. I worked near a woman who whined (supposedly to herself, but I could plainly hear her) all day long. It was like standing next to someone who was running her fingernails up and down a chalkboard all the time. I wasn't even aware of the underlying tension it was causing until she was gone for a few days and I realized I had relaxed.

No job is perfect. And believe me, as long as we work with other people, no coworker is perfect. There are inequities. Sometimes the inequities benefit the other person. But if we are truthful, sometimes the inequities benefit us.

If we want to complain, there is always something to complain about. But this kind of whining gets us nowhere. Better to devise a plan of action that works and then confront the issue head-on.

My company recently moved to a new campus, leaving about a hundred of us behind at the old site. Rapid growth had made it impossible for the entire staff to move to the new site. That was all right with those of us left behind. We understood. But the administration was so consumed with getting everyone settled at the new campus that they forgot us.

I did pretty well the first couple of weeks until I realized there were stacks of trash, papers, and miscellaneous stuff the departing staff had left behind. I said to my secretary, "I've had it. Get someone on the phone and see what we have to do to get this place cleaned up."

It wasn't my job to confront the situation. It wasn't my job to do it, but I rolled up my sleeves and plunged into the mess in the coffee area and straightened it up. It took about six or eight phone calls to get someone in authority to realize they'd left us with no toilet paper or paper towels in the bathrooms, unemptied wastepaper baskets, and carpets that hadn't been vacuumed in weeks. Within a couple of hours, things were humming as workmen scurried to haul the trash out. Soon the head of building maintenance was at my desk saying, "Tell everyone we'll try to do better."

In this case, the administration truly didn't realize the situation with which we'd been left. Whining would never have accomplished anything but lowering the morale of the rest of the staff. A plan of action that leaves no room for whining and deals with the situation and makes it better is the only thing that works.

JOKING AND PLAYING TRICKS

Joking and playing tricks are part of office life. Probably little harm is done when the jokes or stunts are done in moderation and with taste. But jokes that are at the expense of other people or that border on sexual harassment are not funny and need to be confronted.

Inappropriate stunts can be as simple as taking someone's equipment so she can't do the job properly, or they can be real setups that embarrass the worker to the point that she is unable to perform her task because of emotional distress. If it happens to you, you need to make a quick assessment. Is this just for fun, or is it malicious? If it's for fun, just laugh and watch for a chance to have some fun yourself. If it's malicious, then take it up with someone in leadership and make sure it is stopped before it gets out of hand.

AUTHORITARIAN OR PATRONIZING COWORKERS

These are at opposite ends of the spectrum of relationships, and both are maddening.

Authoritarians always have the right procedure, the right answer, the right tool. There is no other way to do a task besides their way. How you relate to them depends on their position. If the person is the boss, you are going to have to listen and try to implement what he or she is asking. If the person is a coworker, you're probably still going to have to listen and then decide whether it is worth it to confront the issue. Otherwise you'll have to ignore it or somehow downplay the pushing and controlling. It's difficult to relate to such a person no matter what his status.

The patronizer is equally maddening. Who wants to be treated like a child? Patronizing is a form of control, a way of keeping another in her place. Women are just as capable as men of patronizing their coworkers. Patronizing is demeaning to the one being patronized. And, done deliber-

I vent my feelings to a trusted, noninvolved friend. —*Kristine*

ately, it is meant to be just that. But it is not always done deliberately. Sometimes the patronizer thinks she is being kind. It is a kindness given where it is not needed and not asked for. It is false kindness.

This is an issue that needs to be confronted directly with the patronizer. It could be that the person is not aware of what he or she is doing, and telling the person how it makes you feel might be all that's needed. More than likely, though, it is a lifelong pattern, and it will be necessary for you to point out patronizing when it is taking place, many times, before the person gets the message. After a while the patronizer may begin to see what it is that angers you and others.

Patronizing is just as demeaning and disruptive in the workplace as authoritarianism. Neither one is healthy. Don't allow either to continue.

GOSSIP

That insidious, pervasive destroyer of office morale—gossip—is fun, and we all indulge in it to one degree or another. It may start as a rumor, be escalated to gossip, and end up as libelous, destructive information.

Have you ever noticed that there seem to be people around an office that know everything that's going on with regard both to the business and to everyone's personal life?

We need to take a good hard look at our involvement in office talk and determine the point at which passing along necessary information becomes gossip. We need to think about information that helps and information that destroys. We need to ask ourselves, How would I feel if this information were being passed around about me? Do you really need to tell someone else what you've just heard about a coworker?

Glynis Breakwell says in her book *The Quiet Rebel:*

> Once loose in an organization, a rumor is as difficult to control as a plague of locusts. The dominant rumors can set the tone for the entire workplace: redundancy rumors can stunt productivity growth; rumors of mergers can produce panic withdrawal of funds, etc. The longevity of a rumor and its power to upset the balance of the workplace ambience depend very much upon how close it is to the central concerns of the majority of people working there, and upon how far it can be countermanded by fact.[3]

It isn't easy, but the only way to stop destructive gossip is to stop listening to and passing along rumors. When you do that, you are setting yourself apart from the crowd, and it is possible that you yourself will become grist for the rumor mill.

Those who set themselves apart from gossip, who don't divulge a lot of information about their private lives, who confront gossip and other negative office practices, are surely setting themselves up for conflict either overtly or covertly. But it is the better way to work, the better way to live—and it is the way that enables you to look in the mirror at the end of the day and know you've been a good and faithful employee and servant of the Lord.

The bottom line in dealing with any relational problems in an office setting is that we must think before we speak or act. We don't want to be part of the problem, but part of the

I address the issue at hand as soon as possible so no problem has time to brew or fester. —*Bettina*

solution. We must be aware that our attempts to change the system might have a high price tag attached. We need to know that when we confront injustice and poor workplace practices, the going could get pretty rough. Old systems don't come down easily. But if we can make the workplace even one iota better for ourselves or for our coworkers, then we have done a good thing.

SUGGESTED READING

Constance Backhouse, *Sexual Harassment on the Job: How to Avoid the Working Woman's Nightmare* (Englewood Cliffs, N.J.: Prentice Hall, 1981).

Ellen Bravo and Ellen Cassedy, *The Nine to Five Guide to Combating Sexual Harassment* (New York: Wiley, 1992).

Glynis M. Breakwell, *The Quiet Rebel* (New York: Grove, 1985).

Emily B. Kirby, *Yes, You Can: The Working Woman's Guide to Her Legal Rights, Fair Employment, and Equal Pay* (Englewood Cliffs, N.J.: Prentice Hall, 1984).

Muriel Solomon, *Working with Difficult People* (Englewood Cliffs, N.J.: Prentice Hall, 1990).

Susan L. Webb, *Step Forward: Sexual Harassment in the Workplace* (New York: MasterMedia, 1991).

Mary Whelchel, *The Christian Working Woman* (Grand Rapids: Baker, 1988). Chapters 8 and 9 especially pertain to these issues.

Jerry Wisinski, *Resolving Conflicts on the Job* (New York: AMACOM, 1993).

CHAPTER 11

Watch Out for the Danger Zone

G ood night, Cherise! Don't work too late," Sandy called as she turned out the lights in the outer office.

"I just have to finish this report. I shouldn't be too long." But her secretary knew that Cherise would still be working at eight, just as she did every night—except for her "late" nights.

Sandy shook her head as she left the building, wondering what kind of home life Cherise had. How much could her husband stand until he'd had enough? Do her children even know her?

Cherise may not know it, but she is an addict—just as surely as any alcoholic or any pill-popping street junkie. She exhibits the same characteristics as a woman who compulsively shops, spends, binges, or gambles. She is as tied to her addiction as a chain-smoker is to hers. The big difference is that Cherise's addiction is approved by the majority of people and is encouraged by the companies for which we work. Her addiction is *work*.

Yes, work! Because we want to do a good job, because we need to get ahead, because we think it is expected of us,

I love to ride horses, and I jump horses over fences. It takes all my focus because if I don't focus it will be dangerous.

—Kathleen

many of us (yes, I'm including myself) work in a compulsive manner. If you are not one of us, then you might want to skip this chapter. That is, unless you know a work addict—or even live with one.

In most of the organizations where I've worked, arriving early, staying late, working through lunch hours, taking work home, and working on weekends have been admired. It hasn't mattered that spouses grew angry with the program, people eventually had to take six-week stress breaks, children felt neglected, and stress-related illnesses attacked the worker. All of that was overlooked while we all viewed the wonderful achievements, the "ministry" that was being done.

There is something terribly wrong with this picture, and we need to take a good, hard look at it. In my own case, work addiction was a direct result of my low self-esteem. I was trying so hard to prove myself that I almost totally burned myself out. It wasn't until I dragged the hollow shell of what I had become to a counselor's office that I began to unravel the very complex work addiction I had acquired. And unraveling it took a long time.

As with any addiction, it is easy for me to fall back into the trap. I have to fight back, watch for tendencies, realize I'm working too hard for the wrong reasons. I know I will fight work addiction for the rest of my life. And sometimes now the pendulum swings too far the other way. I overreact when someone suggests we might have to work over a weekend to finish a project. I overreact when the deadlines are pushing down on me. I overreact when someone criticizes the way in which I am doing my work.

It's a subtle addiction. No one finds you bombed out of your head with drugs or falling down drunk in a corner. But it's as real an addiction as any of the others, and the war to overcome it is, in many ways, just as tough.

ARE YOU ADDICTED TO WORK?

I can just hear you saying, "I love my work. I'm good at it. What's wrong with work?" There's *nothing* wrong with work. We all have to do it. The problem comes from what drives us to work and the way in which we approach it. Here are some symptoms work addicts might experience on a regular basis:[1]

PHYSICAL SYMPTOMS
- Headaches
- Fatigue
- Allergies
- Indigestion
- Stomachaches
- Ulcers
- Chest pain
- Shortness of breath
- Nervous tics
- Dizziness

BEHAVIORAL SYMPTOMS
- Temper outbursts
- Restlessness
- Insomnia
- Difficulty relaxing
- Hyperactivity
- Irritability and impatience
- Forgetfulness
- Difficulty concentrating
- Boredom
- Mood swings (from euphoria to depression)

Brian Robinson has written a very fine book entitled *Work Addiction,* in which he presents the following quiz to measure work compulsion. He calls it a Work Addiction Risk Test (WART).

WART (WORK ADDICTION RISK TEST)
Read each of the twenty-five statements below and decide how much each one pertains to you. Using the rating scale of 1 (never true), 2 (seldom true), 3 (often true), and 4 (always true), put the number that best fits you in the blank beside each statement.

_____ 1. I prefer to do things myself rather than ask for help.
_____ 2. I get very impatient when I have to wait for someone else or when something takes too long, such as long, slow-moving lines.
_____ 3. I seem to be in a hurry and racing against the clock.

_____ 4. I get irritated when I am interrupted
while I am in the middle of something.

_____ 5. I stay busy and keep many irons in the
fire.

_____ 6. I find myself doing two or three things at
one time, such as eating lunch and writing
a memo while talking on the telephone.

_____ 7. I overly commit myself by biting off more
than I can chew.

_____ 8. I feel guilty when I am not working on
something.

_____ 9. It is important that I see the concrete results of what I do.

_____ 10. I am more interested in the final result of
my work than in the process.

_____ 11. Things just never seem to move fast
enough or get done fast enough for me.

_____ 12. I lose my temper when things don't go my
way or work out to suit me.

_____ 13. I ask the same question over again, without realizing it, after I've already been
given the answer once.

_____ 14. I spend a lot of time mentally planning
and thinking about future events while
tuning out the here and now.

_____ 15. I find myself continuing to work after my
coworkers have called it quits.

_____ 16. I get angry when people don't meet my
standards of perfection.

_____ 17. I get upset when I am in situations where
I cannot be in control.

_____ 18. I tend to put myself under pressure with self-imposed deadlines when I work.

_____ 19. It is hard for me to relax when I'm not working.

_____ 20. I spend more time working than on socializing with friends, on hobbies, or on leisure activities.

_____ 21. I dive into projects to get a head start before all the phases have been finalized.

_____ 22. I get upset with myself for making even the smallest mistake.

_____ 23. I put more thought, time, and energy into my work than I do into my relationships with my spouse and family.

_____ 24. I forget, ignore, or minimize important family celebrations such as birthdays, reunions, anniversaries, or holidays.

_____ 25. I make important decisions before I have all the facts and have a chance to think them through thoroughly.

After you have responded to all the statements, add up the numbers in the blanks for your total score. A score from 25–54 is a low-risk score and indicates the absence of any compulsive work behaviors. You have few or none of the risk behaviors that could cause you physical or psychological damage from compulsive working. A low score in this range means you have healthy work habits and have achieved a good balance between work and other areas in your life.

A score of 55–69 means that you are somewhat dependent on your work for something that you are not getting in other areas of your life. You have some, but not all, of the risk behaviors that could cause you physical and psychological harm. It could mean that you are building up to compulsive work habits that could become serious in years to come.

A score of 70–100 means that you are highly addicted to work and that you have all or most of the traits that put you at psychological and physical risk. A high score could mean that relationships with your spouse and friends are threatened, that you have already lost friends, or that a marriage or love relationship has dissolved because of your addiction to work. Your high-risk score also puts you at greater risk for stress-related health problems (such as heart problems or high blood pressure) and psychosomatic illnesses (such as headaches, stomachaches, allergies, or chest pain).[2]

If the results of this test scare you or make you feel defensive, then this chapter is for you. There is not much that is sadder than a worker with hollow eyes, an apathetic approach to life, broken relationships, diminishing work skills, and an inability to remember details. It's particularly sad because it can be prevented.

I get a massage, use the sauna or whirlpool, give myself a facial or a manicure and pedicure, take a bubble bath, read a good novel, or write in my journal. —*Kristine*

WHY DO WE DO IT?

I'm not a trained counselor in the area of work addiction, but I've been a work addict long enough to have a great interest in the subject and to have done a lot of reading about it. It is my observation that work addiction is a symptom of a much deeper problem. One can change behavior—work fewer hours, take vacations, learn to play golf—and still be addicted. Usually a work addict attacks a vacation in the same manner in which she attacks a job. She works at vacationing. She works at golfing. She may be working fewer hours at the job, but she fills up the time with projects at home. Or she may actually do nothing, but the motor is running all the time. She just can't shut down.

Diane Fassel, a management consultant and mediator, says in her book *Working Ourselves to Death*:

> For women and for women workaholics, the issue is not ability. Women tend to be realistic about ability. The issue is belief in themselves. . . . Workaholism worms its way right into that place in us where we feel we aren't good enough. It tries to fill a void externally through relentless busyness.

A friend once observed that "work is the addiction of choice of the unworthy. . . ." Our sense of self is not separate from our achievements; rather it actually depends upon achievements.[3]

In *The Indispensable Woman*, Ellen Sue Stern says that we try to increase our self-esteem by becoming indispensable. Women have always been the nurturers of family life, but this goes way beyond nurturing. Stern says:

> Our unconscious goal is to be so desirable, so smart, so competent, so giving, so perfect that others will be

convinced they can't get along as well, if at all, without us. In our efforts to guarantee career security and advancement, to hold on to our relationships, and mostly, to create and maintain a positive image of ourselves, we pretend we are infallible and that nothing is beyond our scope.[4]

For me, all of the above was true. Once a friend asked me, "What drives you, Gwen?" At that time I was at the height of my addiction, and I honestly didn't know what was driving me. There was a tremendous need to prove my worth to the organization for which I was working. There was a need to be the best at everything I attempted. There was denial that something was wrong in my closest relationships—there couldn't be; everything had to be perfect.

What was driving me? Some frenetic need to prove my worth by what I could accomplish. It wasn't until exhaustion, depression, and total burnout hit with full force that I knew I had to find answers. And I discovered exactly what you've read above: that I was bolstering my shredded self-esteem by achieving a lot through my work.

I remember times when something would go wrong on the job, and instead of confronting it and the unrealistic expectations of supervisors, I'd determine to work harder and make it better. I would get so exhausted, so numb, that I sometimes felt like two people, one watching the other perform.

But through counseling, coming to understand that my relationships were not what I had supposed, confronting my own pain and need, I finally began to realize that I am not what I do; I am who I am apart from any performance.

restyle a room, dig in the garden, or window shop at a different mall from the one where I usually go.

— Patricia

Do you have any idea how freeing that is? That acceptance of self opens a whole world of possibilities—including employment possibilities, because you don't have to do what you've always done to prove yourself. I could work as a clerk in a grocery store. Clerks in grocery stores have great value and worth. I could work as a highway flagger. It's a job of importance. I could scrub toilets for a living. We all need people who do that! I could take a year off (if I could afford it) and do nothing—and still have great value because I am not what I do; I am who I am.

HOW DO I START TO RECOVER?

The very first step is to stop the denial. All addictions rest firmly on denial. If you have questions about whether you are a work addict or not, ask those closest to you. They know. And if they have not been intimidated by you and your addiction, they will tell you the truth, for our work addiction impacts those around us.

My children tried to tell me. They'd say, "Mom, just stop working and listen to me." I'd try to stop, but soon I'd find a dishcloth and begin wiping the cupboard tops while I listened. It was very frustrating to them. I'd also jump ahead of them and assume I knew what they were going to tell me. I'd finish sentences for them.

We cannot begin to recover from work addiction until we are willing to admit we *are* work addicts. We have to face the fact that there is something wrong in our lives and we are using work to cover it up. We have to acknowledge that *we* might be the problem in our failing relationships.

There's only one path to take, and that is a path of confronting our work addiction honestly. The path leads right up the middle of our pain. It takes tremendous courage to look ourselves full in the face and admit what we are. It's not an easy path, but it will bring us to a new day, a better way of life.

REALIZE RECOVERY IS A PROCESS

When I first went to see a counselor I asked, "How long will this take?"—a typical question from a work addict. I didn't want to hear that it might take years. I didn't want to know that it was a process. I just wanted to get better and get on with life.

Work addicts want it fixed—and right now. The way in which we have moved toward goals has always been *see it and charge*. Unfortunately, recovery from any addiction is not quite that simple. It takes time to unravel the complex tangle of our lives and see what's driving us to consume ourselves with work.

GET PROFESSIONAL HELP

Most of us cannot see ourselves for what we are, and those with whom we have day-to-day relationships are too subjective to truly help us. For that reason, we need someone skilled, caring, compassionate, objective, and confronting to help us.

Get help from some kind of professional Christian counselor. Check into your insurance program and see what benefits are offered for mental health care. It probably won't cover the entire cost, and counseling can be expensive. It was difficult for me to spend the amount of money required to get professional help. But friends who'd been through the process reminded me that I'm not very good to myself. I haven't known how to take care of myself. And so, mostly on their recommendation, I spent the money. I made the investment in myself and my future. Decide now that you are worth whatever it costs to unravel the tangles in your life that are causing workaholism and other addictions.

Just a word about selecting a counselor: My success in finding the right counselor has come from recommendations of friends. I also believe that God saw my desperate need and led me to the right counselors at the right time. You may not mesh with a counselor and may have to try several before you find one with whom you can work. That's important, because recovery is hard work.

TURN TO GOD

Every book I have read on the subject of addictions, whether from a Christian or secular perspective, says that ultimately addictions are a spiritual problem. At some point in recovery we have to give up our own ability to cope with the problem and throw ourselves upon the mercy of a "higher power." It's the basis of The Twelve Steps program of Alcoholics Anonymous and all the programs modeled after it. We cannot conquer addictions by ourselves. We have to turn to God for his help. We have to give up.

If you are struggling with work addiction and are ready to stop denying it, turn to God and ask his help for the tough journey to recovery.

LEARN TO RELAX

At some place and time in our lives, we have to finally admit that the world does not revolve around what we do and don't do. No person is indispensable. We have to give ourselves permission to relax—to stop working.

There is nothing wrong with taking care of yourself. When you do, you have more to give back to your family, your job, your community, your church, and yourself.

Part of relaxing is learning to pamper yourself from time to time. Doesn't that sound nice? Most work addicts know very little about pampering themselves. Here are some ideas to get you started:

- Go to a favorite coffee shop with a good book and just relax.
- Go for a jog or a swim, maybe even in the middle of the day.
- Get a bike and ride it often.
- Play with your children and pretend you are a child too.
- Read the Sunday paper all the way through without getting up to do something.
- Join a bird-watching club.
- Plant a flower bed and spend a few minutes every day tending it. (Don't make it work—make it fun.)
- Take long, hot bubble baths and don't allow interruptions.
- Go to breakfast with your husband or a friend twice a week.
- Spend your lunch hour browsing in a bookshop.
- Have a massage.

- Soak in a hot tub.
- Get away for a weekend and do absolutely nothing.
- Take a cruise or some other kind of wonderful vacation.
- Join an aerobics class.
- Learn to paint.
- Have long telephone talks with a friend.
- Write in a journal about all the good things that are happening to you.
- Put fresh flowers on your desk once a week.
- Watch a spectacular sunrise or sunset from beginning to end.
- Stargaze and remember how insignificant most things we are striving to do really are.
- Curl up in front of the fire with a cup of hot cider and a book you've been dying to read.
- Have your hair done by a professional who will take time with you.
- Have your nails or toenails done.
- Buy a dress that makes you look smashing.
- Sit quietly in a church and contemplate God's goodness to you.

WORK IN MODERATION

There is always more work to be done. No matter how much you do, there is always more. And surprisingly, most of it will keep. We have to tell ourselves, "I'm only going to work two hours, then I'm going for a long, relaxing walk."

Most of us work addicts don't even think of setting a time limit. We start and we keep going until the job is done, be that one hour or ten. But if we are to recover, we have to set limits on ourselves.

Another question I had for my counselor was "But I love my work. Do I have to stop working?" She smiled gently at me and said, "No, but your working will come from a different place inside you." I didn't understand what she was saying—she might just as well have been speaking Chinese to me. I know now. I work hard because I want to do a good job for my company and for my Lord. But I don't work to prove who I am. When I leave work, I can put it completely out of my mind. I can actually take a walk at lunchtime and enjoy what I am seeing instead of rushing to get back to work.

STRENGTHEN RELATIONSHIPS

The families of most work addicts are in trouble. Husbands are tired of taking second place. They're tired of having a wife who collapses from exhaustion, unable to communicate except in terse words. They'd like to have a companion, a lover, a friend with whom to share things—not just an automaton spinning through life.

If the work addict starts taking some of the steps listed previously in this chapter—moderating work, seeking help to find out what's causing the addiction, learning to relax—and if she is honest about her attempts to change, she will find support from her family. They are the most impacted by the work addiction, and they have the most to gain by a change in the addict's life.

Many work addicts are also

I play with my computer or crochet. —*Bonnie*

codependent and, as such, have a difficult time giving responsibility to others in the family. Sharing the workload is one way to teach others responsibility and to lighten the burden on the working wife and mother.

And whether you have a family or not, it's important to have friends outside of work. It's easy to relate to the people with whom we work and not bother to find others with whom to have social contact. But we are seriously limiting ourselves by doing so. And guess what you and your work colleagues talk about? You guessed it—work. It's just more of the same, rehashed.

Reach out. Find other social environments so that work is not the sum total of your life.

CELEBRATE

Celebrate everything. Learn to rejoice over small things. Celebrate the return of the robin, the first snow, the turn of the seasons, special days, unspecial days.

I have a flag I put out frequently at my house. Friends have said, "What's the occasion? Did I miss something?"

"No," I tell them, "I just like the way my house looks with a flag flying out front."

Someday I'd like to have some banners to fly as a greeting to guests, to celebrate special days, to just enjoy.

VALIDATE YOURSELF

Keep the little notes friends send you, the kudos, the mementos that bring a warm feeling. Take them out from time to time and remember what really matters. Is this job, this work, the most important thing in life? No, it's not. Keep perspective by taking time to think about what has meaning for you.

SUGGESTED READING

Diane Fassel, *Working Ourselves to Death: The High Cost of Workaholism and the Rewards of Recovery* (San Francisco: HarperSanFrancisco, 1992).

Archibald D. Hart, *Adrenalin and Stress* (Dallas: Word, 1991).

Bryan E. Robinson, *Work Addiction: Hidden Legacies of Adult Children* (Deerfield Beach, Fla.: Health Communications, 1989).

Marsha Sinetar, *Do What You Love, the Money Will Follow: Discovering Your Right Livelihood* (New York: Dell, 1989). Chapter 9 especially deals with this topic.

Nina Tassi, *Urgency Addiction: How to Slow Down without Sacrificing Success* (New York: NAL-Dutton, 1993).

*Thriving through
Stress Reduction*

CHAPTER 12

Growing Spiritually

y survey of working women held a wonderful
surprise. Many more working women were involved in some kind of Bible study than I would
have imagined. I thought working women, as a whole,
would be too busy to include Bible study in their lives. But
I was wrong.

The truly successful working woman knows that her
strength lies not in her skills or knowledge, her working
relationships or expertise, but in her relationship to Christ.

I've observed some of the women with whom I work.
Even though we're working in a ministry that makes daily
devotions a part of our schedule, these women sneak off at
lunchtime with their Bibles. I know others are involved in
Bible study groups and prayer fellowships. I know many
listen to tapes of encouraging speakers in their cars on their
way to work. I know they've found the source of their
strength—their ability to thrive—in their relationship with
Christ.

I once heard about a concert violinist who said, "If I don't
practice for a day, I know it. If I don't practice for two days,
my audience knows it, and if I don't practice for three days,

You can't give to others if you don't have anything inside yourself, so take time for yourself.

—Marie

the whole world knows it." It isn't much different in our walk with Christ. We need daily contact with the source of our strength and life. Miss one day and you know something's amiss. Miss two days and your work companions know it. Miss a week or more, and the whole office will probably know it.

I DON'T HAVE THE TIME

It's probably true from a natural standpoint that none of us has time to just sit and read and think, but we have to consider what's important versus what's urgent. Our relationship with Christ is important—more important than those things that call to you saying "do me" or "fix me."

Last summer I took a trip to Yellowstone Park with a young friend, and I learned something important from her. Jennifer had a small devotional book and Bible with her. On the first morning we sat just above Yellowstone Falls and read together from this very brief devotional guide, and then we read a Scripture passage. Following that we each silently prayed, rejoiced in the beauty we were seeing, and went on our way for the day.

What I learned was that I often try to do more in my devotional time than I have time for. I feel I have to read x number of Scripture verses (or chapters!) and pray a certain amount of time. What happens is that it becomes threatening—too time consuming. As a result, I delay it and sometimes don't ever get to it. This is definitely a case where less is more. Just turning toward God in a simple, unassuming way, acknowledging his presence in our lives, and asking his guidance for the day is a sufficient start. A simple approach to our devotional time will create a hunger for God within us, and we'll find ourselves spending more time with the Lord—and it won't be a duty.

BIBLE STUDY IS AN AVENUE TO GROWTH

For a number of years I've been concerned about where working women are getting their spiritual training. Before we were working full-time, we went to morning Bible studies and daytime women's groups. We were involved in Sunday school, either as teachers or as students. But when so many hours of our week are taken up with employment and all that goes with living, it's easy to ignore our need for spiritual training.

Most of us make it to a Sunday morning church service, but how much actual training goes on there? Sunday morning services tend to be inspirational, and while we all need inspiration, we also need spiritual meat to chew on.

We have to be self-motivated, and we will only become motivated as we see our own need. We have to be convinced that we cannot operate from a Christian perspective in our workplace when we are operating out of an empty life. Harold Lindsell, a well-known Christian writer and publisher, once said, "What's in the well comes up in the bucket." You can't draw water from an empty well.

The problem for us in many cases is not a lack of awareness about our spiritual need. Indeed, most of us feel guilty about our lack of Bible study and prayer. The problem is usually lack of time and energy. Perhaps we would like to meet with other women in a Bible study, but there simply isn't time to do that and still take care of a family.

Remember what I said earlier: Keep it simple. Just build a little each day. Like my friend Jennifer, do a little, and do it every day. There is scriptural verification for such a plan. "For we are . . . God's building. According to the grace of God which was given to me, as a wise master builder I laid a foundation, and another is building upon it. But let each man [or woman] be careful how he builds upon it" (1 Corinthians 3:9-10).

The school district is building a new junior high school near me. It is a brick structure. And I've observed that it is being built by laying one brick at a time and putting up one joist at a time. And if you keep doing that long enough, eventually you have a strong building. Never underestimate the power of adding one truth, one principle, one insight at a time to your life. Before you know it, you'll have a strong fortress of spiritual strength in your life.

Satan would love to convince us that we need to be spending half an hour (or more) in personal Bible study every day, meeting with a Bible study group once a week, and attending a Sunday school class. He has a way of telling us that if we can't do that, we're failing, and we might just as well give up and do nothing. If he can convince us of this lie, he knows he's got us. Don't listen to him. He's the destroyer of our souls. It is the Word of God that keeps us out of Satan's clutches. It is truth that helps us to resist him so that he will flee from us.

At the end of this chapter are resource materials for personal Bible study. This is only a start. A wise investment in yourself would be to go to a Christian bookstore for an hour and see the kinds of materials that are available.

In looking for resource materials, think about listening to audiocassettes during your commuting time. The entire Bible is available on cassette in several different versions. Reading or listening to straight Scripture, without any commentary or embellishments, is valuable. We need to be careful not to be listening only to tapes of sermons and speeches. If all we listen to are other people's messages, we're getting spiritual food secondhand. Make it a rule to daily go to the source, God himself, and to his Word.

PRAYER AND MEDITATION—AVENUES TO THRIVING

Bible study is one way of thriving spiritually, and prayer and meditation are others. It's possible to pray on the run, and often that's the only thing a busy working woman can do. But it is so much more profitable to stop, slow down, and let the world coast without you while you talk to the Father and he talks to you. There is no way we can process the huge amounts of information that come our way daily unless we stop and think, pray, and meditate.

Maybe it's best stated by the following poem:

He's Calling You Now

Don't tell me why you are late
How the clock stopped
And the phone rang
And the dog got sick
And you couldn't find your keys
And you got lost

And no one knew the street
It's okay
I understand
Just please don't pour all that confusion
Out of your mouth into my head
I have enough of my own
Tell the truth
You are late because you have been playing God again
Just like we all have
Trying to be all things to all people
Trying to control our own life
And the lives of those we love
But I am here to share some Good News
Remember Jesus?
He was never late
Never in a hurry
Now there is a Man Who really knows how to live!
And, how to love
Well, I just heard He did more than die for my sins
The Good News is, He doesn't expect me to try and be like
    Him
No, He came to be me
That's right, be me
That means I can let Him be God
And be me also!
"Just relax," He said
"Enjoy the ride
I'll do the driving, provide the power
And be responsible for us both
Just keep Me company along the way
That's all I ask"

And so I have
And it's a wonderful way to live!
No, on second thought
He's wonderful!
He is the wonder and the joy of it all
And He's been here all along
In me!
Amazing!
But I came to tell you
He's in you also!
Yes, in you!
Listen, don't you hear?
He's calling you now
Waiting to enter that last secret
    chamber of your heart
Oh, friend, let Him in
He comes in as God
But He lives out His life
As you.

—Joan Wilson[1]

And that's about the sum of it. Jesus Christ just wants to live out his life through us; and there's no way he can do that if we are frantically dashing from one thing to the next, trying to be the savior of the world. There's no way we can have the mind of Christ if we don't stop to listen and think and determine what he is saying to us, both through his Word and

This time in your life will not last forever. The family, work, financial difficulties will not have to be withstood for the rest of your life. Try to see it as God does. Know that these are transient occurrences and that his love, his heart will always be open toward you. *—Linda*

through the insights he gives us when we pray and meditate.

Once again, I rather suspect that we are bound by
shoulds, and because we cannot possibly live up to the
shoulds, we give up and don't do anything. Buy up the
minutes. What about commuting time? Sometimes our car
is the only place we are alone all day long. Or what about
the train or bus you ride to work? Invest in a little cassette
player. Buy some worship music tapes. Have your prayer
list with you, and use those minutes — minutes that could be
consumed in boredom and frustration — to commune with
your heavenly Father. Here are some more ideas for snatch-
ing precious time with the Lord:

- Sneak away at lunchtime to a church or a park
  and renew your mind through communion with
  God. Or take a walk — alone — and talk with him.
- Get up a few minutes earlier than everyone else
  and talk with him as you have that first cup of tea
  or coffee.
- Find a bite of time during those first few minutes
  when you return from work. During your reentry
  time, stop for a few minutes and acknowledge his
  presence with you.

There's a way to find time to talk to God. We just have
to look for it. We have to be careful that the enemy of our
soul — Satan — doesn't convince us we're too busy or that
we aren't doing it right. Jesus Christ is our very best friend,
and Satan will do everything he can to keep us away from

that relationship because he knows it means death to his influence in our lives.

YOU CAN BE AN EFFECTIVE WITNESS

Another area of great concern to most Christians is that of being an effective witness. Never, never, never underestimate the power of a life lived quietly and consistently for the Lord. That is the most powerful witness of all. Your fellow workers are watching your response to stressful situations. They notice the lack of expletives in your language. Your concern for others is obvious. It is out of the context of your life, lived consistently before your fellow workers, that the opportunities to speak for Christ will come.

There are some programs and ideas to help us be confident when presenting the gospel, which are helpful but not necessarily the most effective way. The best witness comes out of our relationship with Jesus. You can tell when someone is in love. It shows, even if that person doesn't tell you she is in love. The same goes for our relationship with Jesus. If we are in love with him, it shows. We might hear, "Something's different about you. What is it?" At that point, the door is open to simply tell the inquirer about our love life with Jesus.

Once again, the enemy of our soul will try to tell us we don't do it well. He'll convince us we'll botch the opportunity. He binds us up in fear and zips our mouths shut, rendering us useless as witnesses.

Want to know something wonderful? There is no wrong way to witness. The Holy Spirit takes our best efforts and

*D*on't let other working women or Christians impose upon you a sense of what you should be doing. God wants you to be who you are.

—Janet

perfects them. It is he who does the life-changing work, not us.

Have you ever prepared a wonderful speech, either formally or informally, and just known that what you were saying had great life-changing value and then discovered later that it was some aside you had thrown into the talk that touched a life? Frustrating, isn't it?

We need to relax, let go, and, as the poem above said, stop "playing God." Let God be God, and let him live out his life through us. Let the river of his love and grace flow straight through us and out onto the parched land of our workplace. Let our love and concern, our tenderness and caring, our compassion and truthfulness bear witness to the love of Christ in us. It is tremendously appealing!

WORK AS AN ACT OF DEVOTION

In this book we've talked about work as an addiction, work as a passion, and work as a necessity, but there is another side to work, too. That is work as an act of devotion. It is a devotion given to employers, to those we care about, to God, to the ongoing work of the kingdom of God, and last, but not least, to ourselves.

If work flows out of a well-integrated personality, if work fits the worker, if there is a high sense of value of the work, if there is a calling to work, then work and play are indistinguishable from each other and work is something we do to express our caring for others and for ourselves.

That's a lot of ifs, and we don't achieve them easily. In fact, most of us never start on the road to resolving work conflicts and personal conflicts. We drag ourselves to jobs we hate, because we are afraid to change. We are afraid to risk losing what we have to obtain something better.

But think of some of the "greats" of history and the passion with which they went to their work. Think of Michelangelo lying on his back painting the Sistine Chapel. His was a work of devotion. Think of Mozart, who literally burned himself out with his passion for his work. Think of Louis Pasteur, Madame Curie, Einstein, Schweitzer, and thousands of others who gave themselves to their work and in the process gave us wonderful gifts to better our lives.

I'm a book editor when I'm not writing my own books. For some, the thought of book editing seems a laborious, boring, tedious job. I don't see it that way. I'm always looking for the next book that will bring help and hope to its readers. I'm trying to help the authors get their passion, their message across in the best way possible. I'm trying to make the books so reader friendly that a potential reader, instead of being repulsed by line upon line of text ("too hard, too complicated; I don't have time to read this"), finds herself pulled into it ("hmmm; this is interesting, doesn't look too hard; I think I can find time to read this").

My work is my passion. I love it. I would rather do what I do than anything else I can think of. I get tired of going to work, just like everyone else, but it has little to do with the job itself. I just get physically tired. But even though I'm tired, today I might find another great book idea that will change someone's life forever.

Marsha Sinetar says:

> Work becomes a devotion, a labor of love, and indeed—whatever the person himself might call it—a spiritual exercise because the individual's concentrative powers, his choices, actions and values, are motivated, prompted and fueled by love, and his service, as it were, is simply the enactment of this positive lifeforce. His being or essential self lives in all he does.
>
> The vocationally integrated person does not long for love; he has it. He does not yearn for happiness; he has it. He does not strive for completion, finality, satisfaction: he has these, and he has qualities in the very act and process of doing the work he enjoys."[2]

We are fearfully, wonderfully, and complexly made. Each part of our life affects another. When we deal with the issues of our life, when we say no to toxic or spirit-breaking relationships, we can then begin to love others and to know what kind of work we love, the kind of work to which we are best suited. Then work can become an act of devotion.

KEEPING A JOURNAL AS AN AVENUE TO STRESS REDUCTION

Keeping a personal journal is a proven technique to help us when we are feeling confused. When we are under stress, our thoughts tend to spiral, and each time our thoughts pass one of those spirals, they pick up a little more frustration and lose a little more objectivity about our situation. But writing down what's going on inside helps us uncoil our thoughts. It slows down our thought process so that we can see what's happening in our mind. It forces us to be honest with ourselves.

Our journal must be completely private so that we can be completely honest. Our healing from stress is in some measure going to be related to our level of honesty.

A humorous aside is the little poem that says:

> *Now I lay me down to sleep.*
> *I pray the Lord my soul to keep.*
> *If I should die before I wake,*
> *Please throw my journals in the lake.*

A journal can be as plain as a yellow pad or spiral notebook. You don't need a fancy blank book. In fact, a fancy blank book might cause you to write in a stilted manner rather than helping you really express your inner thoughts and feelings.

You don't have to journal every day. You can if you wish, but this is not a rule by which to be bound. Your journal is a tool to help you handle tension, sorrow, stress, emotional pain. It's also a place to record your successes, your joys, your insights.

Gabriele Rico, a well-known writer, educator, and editorial advisor, has written a rather complicated but thorough book on the subject of journalizing. She says:

> Learning to express our all-too-often amorphous mass of feelings is a constructive, creative act. It taps your potential for regaining balance; it allows for the

emergence of patterns of feeling. It alerts you to the power of change coming from within, leading you from hurt to health, from numbness to vitality, from pain to possibility.[3]

And then Gabriele tells of her own experience:

> I learned early to deny my feelings. It was many years before I unlearned that impulse. As an adult I thought, "If only I try harder, work longer, pretend I'm not having bad feelings, I can contain them." In fact, I was so out of touch with my emotions, I believed I could actually avert crises. So I denied. I denied again and again, until I no longer knew how to disentangle my real feelings from my pretend feelings. The more intense my moments of high emotion, the more energy I spent suppressing them.
>
> What I finally learned seems obvious in retrospect. Feelings are signposts; you are supposed to pay attention to them. To deny them is to deny your self. I learned you can neither run away from your feelings nor from the problems that have generated them.[4]

So out of her own need, where most of us begin, Rico wrote her book. She suggests drawing (scribbling may be a better word) what's going on inside, since in a difficult time most of us don't understand what's going on inside well enough to put it into words. If you are struggling and know that keeping a journal might help, you may want to take a look at her book.

The more I learn about the human body, mind, soul, and

spirit, the more I realize how intertwined they are and how when one area is hurting, the whole person suffers. We were made to have fellowship with God, and if we are not doing that we have put a part of our being on a starvation diet. It will affect everything we are and do. The choice is ours, whether to spend time with him or not. Dear working friend, how will you choose?

SUGGESTED DEVOTIONAL GUIDES

Janet C. Bly, *When Your Marriage Disappoints You* (Colorado Springs: NavPress, 1990).

Alice Chapin, *Three Hundred and Sixty-Five Bible Promises for Busy People* (Wheaton, Ill.: Tyndale House, 1992).

Gloria Chisholm, *When You Can't Get Along* (Colorado Springs: NavPress, 1990).

Judith Couchman, *Lord, Have You Forgotten Me?* (Dallas: Word, 1992).
Lord, Please Help Me to Change (Dallas: Word, 1992).
Getting a Grip on Guilt (Colorado Springs: NavPress, 1990).
Why Is Her Life Better than Mine? (Colorado Springs: NavPress, 1991).

Nancy Groom, *Nobody's Perfect, So Why Do I Try to Be?* (Colorado Springs: NavPress, 1990).

Madalene Harris, *You're Better than You Think* (Colorado Springs: NavPress, 1990).

Sue Monk Kidd, *When the Heart Waits: Spiritual Direction for Life's Sacred Questions* (San Francisco: HarperSanFrancisco, 1992).

Dean Merrill, *Wait Quietly: Devotions for a Busy Parent* (Wheaton, Ill.: Tyndale House, 1994).

Carry a small devotional book or Bible in your purse so you can read in the doctor's office or when waiting in other places. —*Deb*

211

Watchman Nee, *The Joyful Heart* (Wheaton, Ill.: Tyndale House, 1978).

Penelope J. Stokes, *So What If You've Failed?* (Colorado Springs: NavPress, 1990).

David Stoop, and Stephen Arturburn, *The Twelve Step Life Recovery Devotional* (Wheaton, Ill.: Tyndale House, 1993).

Wightman Weese, *The Bible Promise Life Recovery Devotional* (Wheaton, Ill.: Tyndale House, 1992).

Wightman Weese, ed., *A Spiritual Journey Life Renewal Devotional* (Wheaton, Ill.: Tyndale House, 1993).

Also, many denominations have daily devotional guides. Check at your local bookstore.

CHAPTER 13

Healthy Living

Open any current newsstand magazine, and you'll find an article on stress, nutrition, exercise, or all of the above. We are a health-crazed, over-stressed society.

We can't change the way a nation of people live, but we can learn to take care of ourselves. We can learn to eat in a healthy manner, we can learn to get the right amount of exercise, and we can learn to deal with stress. We can thrive!

LEARNING TO READ STRESS SIGNALS

Know yourself. Each person has a slightly different reaction to stress. For me, it's waking in the middle of the night and being unable to go back to sleep. For other women it's migraines and other kinds of headaches, PMS, decreased sex drive, or changes in the menstrual cycle. Left unattended, stress can lead to stroke and heart attack. Stress also lowers the immune system's ability to fight disease.

It's not fair to say that all stress is bad. We need some stress. Stress can drive us forward to achieve. But good stress (eustress) and bad stress (distress) are two different

I **jump rope, use exercise videos, and go swimming.** *—Jan*

things. Good stress gives us a sense of well-being and pushes us forward. Part of the reason eustress is good is that it's not a constant factor in our lives. It excites us for a time then lets us go back to normal. Bad stress, the kind that never lets us rest and recover, can become a killer.

Those who most often have a problem with stress are those with high career goals and high standards for themselves. It's those women who feel that all the problems that happen in life are their fault. It's those who must have and be everything perfect. All you have to do to sign up for a stress attack is to be a full-time working woman, be a full-time wife and mother, and expect everything to be perfect all the time. But there is good news: studies show that juggling a job and family, though stressful, doesn't have to have a negative effect on health—especially for women who have a sense of control at work and who are supported by their families.[1]

There are entire books written on the subject of stress, and you will find reference to these and to a number of magazine articles in the resource section at the end of this chapter.

EXERCISE—YOU CAN LEARN TO LOVE IT!
Wouldn't it be nice if we could sit and look at television exercise programs and feel our muscles tighten? Sorry, friends, it doesn't happen that way. I love the Nike ads that encourage us to Just do it. All the talk about exercise, all the video and other kinds of aerobic classes, all the exercise

equipment available will do us no good unless we "just do it." It's important to find some kind of exercise that truly appeals to you, and then get out there and do it several times a week.

For me it's walking. Walking gets me outdoors, and I love to be outdoors. Being outdoors gets me into the sunshine, which helps fight depression. Walking slows me down to see what's really out there. I see the architecture of the houses on the street. I discover a robin's nest or the first bud in spring or the first leaf to color in the fall. I get to see the sunrise or the sunset in all its majestic beauty. I live on the front range of the Rocky Mountains, near Pike's Peak. I can watch new weather systems boil up over the peak and watch the lightning flash against darkened skies. I get to see the change in water flow in Monument Creek, and once in a while I see a fox running down through the woods near my home.

And best of all, it only costs me the price of a good pair of walking shoes. I keep them under my desk, and many of my coworkers know I'm good for a walk at noon. I often have people come by just before lunch and say, "Want to walk?" I always want to walk! Sometimes I put aside planned errands to walk, and sometimes I make friends walk to the errands with me.

For me, cost is a big factor. I love to swim, so I recently checked out a YMCA near my office. There is a lap-swimming program at noon—perfect. But the price is about forty dollars a month. Right now, that's more than I think I can afford. If I were to spend that amount each month, I'd feel like I had to be at the pool several days a week, and then it would become a duty and not a joy.

In addition to short walks, I also like hiking. Hiking can get you to places most people only dream about. I've stood at the tops of mountains and viewed cirque lakes. I've seen box canyons and fossil beds. I've seen panoramic views that take my breath away. I've walked for hours through silent woods. I've come upon deer grazing in a meadow. I've walked rock-strewn beaches and sandy beaches. I've watched waves crash on both coastlines of America as I've hiked along the tops of sheer rock cliffs.

Well, now you know my passion. What's yours? Do you like bicycling, or is working out in a gym your cup of tea? Do you love tennis or softball, soccer or skating, downhill or cross-country skiing? Or maybe several of these activities interest you. That can be very good because as you tire of one, you can take up another and keep moving.

And that's the most important point of all—keep moving. And there's even more good news. The long-term effect of aerobic exercise—any kind of exercise that gets the body moving and the heart rate up—is that it keeps the body younger. Here are some more ideas to get you thinking:

- *Join a group for walking, hiking, aerobic dancing, or cross-country skiing. Maybe you need the support of others to keep you at it.*
- *Have an outdoor and an indoor activity so that weather cannot be an excuse for not exercising.*
- *Buy a piece of exercise equipment and use it when you can't get outside.*
- *Realize that you need to make a lifelong commitment to exercise.*
- *Remember that exercise is not meant to be a punishment.*

Find something or several somethings you enjoy doing, and do them regularly.

WHAT GOOD WILL IT DO?

Most of us realize that exercise will help us lose weight, but there are a lot of other, possibly more important benefits that you may not be aware of. Here are some of the benefits of regular aerobic exercise (thirty minutes three to five times a week):

- Puts you in a better mood
- Reduces stress and helps you deal with it better
- Burns calories and reduces fat
- Lowers blood pressure
- Reduces the risk of heart disease
- Decreases risk of diabetes
- Reduces cholesterol levels
- Increases level of HDL cholesterol (the good kind)
- Stimulates the bones to produce new cells, lowering the chances of osteoporosis
- Stimulates the immune system to produce antibodies and cells that destroy viruses

There are some studies that show exercise helps us keep a mental edge. This is probably due to the increased flow of blood to the brain. It seems that activities that require thinking with the exercise (tennis vs. riding a stationary bike) even further increase mental agility.

Exercise also increases the level of a chemical called dopamine in our brain. Dopamine is the chemical that causes "runner's high." It makes us feel good, and it prevents the shaking and stiffness that come with aging. It seems that dopamine decreases by about one percent each year after we reach twenty-five years of age. So finding a way to stimulate its production is a good thing.

BETTER LATE THAN NEVER

"But I've never been very active, and it's probably too late," you might be saying. Good news! It's never too late! True, it would have been better if you'd started earlier, but since you didn't, make the best of it. There's a lot to be gained by beginning now.

It may seem frivolous to block out four to six hours a week for yourself to exercise. I struggle to do it all the time. But think of it as an investment—an investment in yourself. You're worth it, and no one is going to take care of you but you.

I read this quote in *Entrepreneurial Woman*, and while it's tongue-in-cheek, it's appropriate in many cases: "If avoiding exercise were an Olympic event, women entrepreneurs would be among the top contenders."[2] That's true not only for women entrepreneurs, but for most women in general.

We all know what happens. The schedule gets tight, and the first thing that's thrown out the window is exercise time. We all do it. So what if you don't have six hours a week? Could you spend twenty minutes a day? If you miss a day—or two or three—be philosophical about it and say, "Today is the first day of the rest of my life. I'll start again today." Don't let discouragement over your lapses keep you sitting. It's all right to have lapses—after all, you are human. Just pick up and keep going.

Face the fact that God made our bodies to move and be used, and most of our lifestyle today keeps us still: office jobs; driving or riding public transportation; sedentary, passive, observing kinds of recreation. We have to overcome our culture and get our bodies moving if they are to work the way God intended.

I promise you that if you start exercising and keep at it faithfully for several months, you *will* feel better.

WHAT YOU EAT HELPS YOU THRIVE

Not only does exercise help you thrive, but what you eat does, too. In saying that, we have to acknowledge that there is a lot of confusing misinformation about food, food additives, vitamins, and herbal medicines. There is a lot we don't know yet. But let's talk about what we do know. We know that excessive fat is bad for us. Breast cancer, heart disease, and many other life-threatening illnesses can be linked to fat consumption.

A good rule of thumb is to consume no more than 33 grams of fat for every 1000 calories. That simply means more vegetables and fruit and less meat. Make meat the side dish and veggies and fruit the main course. Three to six ounces of protein are sufficient for a day. That includes meat, poultry, fish, shellfish, eggs, dried beans and peas, and peanut butter (but remember that peanut butter is also a fat).

Skinless white poultry has 20 percent fewer calories than the same amount of skinless dark poultry and half the fat grams. Crackers, potato chips, and all other kinds of snack chips are loaded with fat. Most dessert foods are loaded with fat—choc-

I walk and do some exercises, but not as much as I should.   *—Lin*

219

olate candy, cakes, cookies, pies, and ice cream.

Watch your intake of salad dressing, margarine, butter, vegetable oils, and nuts. They, too, are loaded with fat. A salad is wonderful food until you add huge amounts of salad dressing. Then it becomes lethal.

Eat whole wheat bread or English muffins without butter or margarine. Use a little jam, jelly, or honey instead; they contain no fat. Look for all-fruit, no-sugar jams. They are wonderful.

Read labels. The number of fat grams is listed on the packaging. Something as innocuous as yogurt may contain eight grams of fat, but a low-fat variety may have only three, and nonfat has none.

The challenge for working women is that in the morning we are too rushed to eat a good breakfast, and in the evenings we collapse. It's so easy to dig into high-fat comfort foods to ease the stress of the day. It adds up to too much fat, poor nutrition, and weight gain.

Watching your fat intake doesn't mean giving up foods you love altogether. It means learning to prepare them in a different way, including cutting down on fatty additions. For instance, baked potatoes have no fat content until you add butter, margarine, sour cream, cheese, bacon bits, etc. The amazing thing is that if you eliminate all the additions, you learn that the potato has a wonderful flavor all its own.

Eat a huge salad of mixed greens. Eat it without dressing, if you can, and learn that lettuce, too, has a flavor of its own. So do spinach, cabbage, broccoli, tomatoes, and cucumbers. If you must put dressing on a salad, use one of the newer delicious nonfat dressings available in supermarkets.

You can make a little dressing go a long way by tossing it with the salad greens instead of pouring it on the top.

Here are some low-fat cooking ideas:

- Whenever possible, roast, bake, or grill meat, poultry, and fish.
- Use ground turkey or extra-lean ground beef instead of regular hamburger.
- Use nonstick cookware or use a vegetable oil spray when frying meat.
- Use a marinade of lemon juice, flavored vinegars, or fruit juices for broiling or tenderizing meats.
- Use low-fat cheese in casseroles, or use just a little very sharp cheese to give more flavor with less cheese.
- Make your own soup stock by boiling meat or poultry bones in water. Let the stock cool, and skim off the fat when it has hardened.
- Stir-fry in a nonstick pan or use a vegetable oil spray.
- Baste meats with homemade stock or broth instead of butter.
- Learn to use lots of herbs for seasonings.
- Use low-fat yogurt in recipes calling for sour cream or mayonnaise. It also makes a great topping for baked potatoes.
- Eat low-fat popcorn as a snack instead of chips.

Eating less fat is one thing each of us can do to help our body. Less fat means less weight, and less weight means the

I try to work out three to five times during the week. On weekends, I try to do some type of physical activity. I also get involved in community sports or church sports.

—Marcella

ability to move with agility. Less fat means cutting down on the possibility of cancer and heart disease.

REVVING UP

Less fat is one dietary thing we can do to help ourselves, but there are others. In doing the research for this chapter, I learned many interesting things about food, and I've done some experimentation. Food can change your mood. Food can rev you up. Food can slow you down.

If you want to rev up, don't reach for coffee, tea, or cola drinks. They will only make you jittery. Reach instead for protein. Protein quells the brain chemical serotonin, the chemical that makes you relaxed and sleepy.

Try:

- Tuna—without mayonnaise
- Low-fat yogurt
- Turkey or lean ham slices
- A hard-boiled egg (but only two or three in a week)
- String cheese
- A lean burger with lots of lettuce and tomatoes

High-carbohydrate foods produce serotonin—the chemical that calms us down. That's why when we are under stress, we often find ourselves reaching for high-carbohydrate foods—chocolate, cookies—and we eat more of them than we would at any other time. If our intake of comfort foods causes weight gain, we are only producing more stress because we're worried about our weight. So here are some ideas for high-carbohydrate, low-fat snacks:

- popcorn
- bagels
- sorbet or sherbet
- English muffins
- breadsticks and whole grain crackers
- pretzels
- pasta with marinara sauce (no meat)
- stir-fried rice and vegetables
- pancakes with fruit and syrup
- baked potato
- split pea soup

Your mother always told you not to go off in the morning without breakfast. Your mother was right. If it's true that our brains function off the nutrients of the food we've eaten, then we have to be eating food. Here are some tips for working women about eating:

- Eat breakfast.
- Eat frequently—some researchers say up to seventeen times a day. Eating small amounts frequently keeps your metabolism up and prevents binge eating.
- Snack on low-fat and, better yet, nonfat foods.

- Keep low-fat, healthy foods in your desk to keep you from putting money in the snack machine.
- Drink lots of water—up to eight glasses (two quarts) a day. Herbal teas or hot water with a twist of lemon will help increase your intake.
- Limit coffee to two cups a day. Caffeine is a diuretic and will drain fluids from your body.
- Keep lunches light. Overeating, particularly carbohydrates, will make you sleepy in the afternoon.
- Instead of eating, take frequent breaks—short walks, stretching exercises—to ease stress.
- Keep the office kitchen stocked with high-energy snacks—nonfat yogurt, low-fat cheeses, single servings of tuna.

WHAT DOES SUPERWOMAN NEED MOST?

Perhaps the most important key to handling the stress of job, home, civic duty, and everything else that goes with life is quality relationships. The loving support of a woman's friends and family can make all the difference in the world. When women were asked if family life was a source of comfort or of stress, 81 percent said it was a source of comfort.[3] Happiness and comfort at home seem to insulate a woman against the stresses of the workplace.

If you're single, you've probably read chapter 5, where we talked a lot about the importance of cultivating a supportive network of friends. If you are in a situation where you don't have family nearby, close friends can make the difference for you. We can't have too many friends, too many good relationships.

Relationships should be give-and-take. Each of us has times when we are strong and can give to our friends and other times when we are weak and need all the help we can get. Many of us need to watch out for codependency: giving of ourselves to others without setting appropriate limits. If we are codependent, we may be attracting other codependent and dependent people. Instead of drawing strength from a relationship, we find we are being sucked dry by it.

I once had a friendship that I am only now able to look at realistically. I dearly loved my friend, and she loved me. She had a complicated life with many problems. I would spend time with her and listen to her problems. I would pray for her and with her and was glad to do it. She was my friend, she needed me, and now I can see that her need of me satisfied some need in my own life. That's codependency. The relationship worked pretty well until I came to a crisis point in my life and I was the one who needed help. Then it fell apart. My friend wasn't able to give to me in the way I had given to her because the relationship hadn't been based on a mutual give-and-take. My new relationships are healthier as I'm learning to deal with my codependent tendencies.

LEARN TO RELAX
We have to learn to relax. Stress makes us want to be on the edge of our chair all the time. Adrenaline causes us to be "on" all the time. Stress and being "on" all the time will wear out the machinery long before it is supposed to be worn out.

Many times the exhaustion we feel has nothing to do with how much work we've done. It's more like revving the engine of an idling vehicle. Getting out for a brisk walk, although physically challenging, can perk you up for the rest of the day.

Is there any animal on earth more relaxed than a cat? My daughter has a big cat—eighteen pounds—with the ridiculous name of Boober. There are few creatures that are more relaxed than Boober. He saves his energy for stalking prey and for playing. The rest of the time, you'll find him curled up in the warmest, most comfortable place he can find.

Have you ever noticed that every time a cat stands up it stretches everything—hind legs extended, back arched, head and neck stretched out as far as they will go? And how does a cat finish its stretch? Usually with an all-over shake. Learn from the cat. Stretch everything many times a day. Look for exercises that can be done sitting right at your desk, or at least standing next to it, that will help relieve stress and energize you.

Healthy living has a tremendous payoff in terms of strength to do your job, emotional health, ability to cope with multiple demands, and a strong sense of self-worth. If you are not living a healthy lifestyle, ask yourself why. Is it a matter of taking time for yourself? (I realize it can be difficult.) Is it a matter of not thinking enough of yourself to do what's best for you? (Doing what's best for you can also be doing what's best for those you love.) Is it a matter of not being willing to invest the money? (It is tough to spend hard-earned dollars on yourself. But you are entitled to use a portion of what you earn to take care of yourself.)

Give yourself, those you love, and those with whom you work a healthy, strong, positive person by investing in a healthy lifestyle.

SUGGESTED READING

Marjorie Blanchard and Mark Tager, *Working Well: Managing for Health and High Performance* (New York: Simon and Schuster, 1985).

Nancy Burstein, *The Executive Body: A Working Woman's Guide to Lifestyle and Total Fitness* (New York: Simon and Schuster, 1984).

Donald T. DeCarlo and Deborah H. Gravenfeld, *Stress in the American Workplace: Alternatives for the Working Wounded* (Fort Washington, Penn.: LRP, 1989).

Robert A. Karasek and Tores Theorell, *Healthy Work: Stress, Productivity, and the Reconstruction of Working Life* (New York: Basic Books, 1990).

Rosalind K. Lording and Herbert A. Otto, ed., *New Life Options: The Working Woman's Resource Book* (New York: McGraw-Hill, 1976).

Pamela Smith, *Eat Well, Live Well* (Lake Mary, Fla.: Creation House, 1992).

Arthur S. Verdesca, *Live, Work, and Be Healthy: A Top Medical Director's Commonsense Advice and Observations for the Working Person* (New York: Van Nostrand Reinhold, 1980).

C. Samuel Verghese, *The Working People's Guide to Stress Management* (Marlton, N.J.: Pain and Stress Management, 1989). Includes information on stress management, stress psychology, stress physiology, stress—the nutritional aspects.

VIDEO

The Working Mom's Survival Guide, Connie Kastelnik (Andover, Mass.: Xenejenex Productions, 1990). This video will help you sort through what's important and what's not when time is your worst enemy. Includes daily aerobic workout, quick makeup tips, and much more.

AUDIOCASSETTE

Bonnie Michaels, *Examining Stress, Guilt and Chaos of Working Parents* (Skokie, Ill.: Parents Resource Network, 1991), audiocassette.

WHERE TO FIND ANSWERS
TO NUTRITIONAL QUESTIONS

Call the National Center for Nutrition and Dietetics,
1-800-366-1655, weekdays between 10:00 A.M. and 5:00 P.M. (EST)
to speak to a nutritionist. Recorded messages are available
twenty-four hours a day.

CHAPTER 14

Learning to Play

I n the last two years I have had two of the most wonderful vacations imaginable. Both were with my adult children. The first was a trip with my son back to the island of Jamaica, where I had spent an internship many years ago. The second, with my daughter, was a whirlwind tour of spots in the Northeast about which authors had written: James Fenimore Cooper's Lake Otsego, Lucy Maud Montgomery's Prince Edward Island, Henry Wadsworth Longfellow's Acadia.

The vacation to Jamaica was extremely laid-back. We spent hours snorkeling, walking beaches, avoiding peddlers, touring small towns and countrysides, and splashing about in waterfalls and surf. I read three just-for-fun books during the week. I also spent hours talking with my son. We ate wonderful food and walked miles and miles.

The other trip was not as restful, but it was exciting and informative, and it gave me and my daughter some time to work on our issues. She learned that when I say I'm hungry, I need to eat fairly soon. I learned that she needs time by herself to absorb what she's seeing and learning. She learned that if I don't get something to eat soon after my announcement, I go a little hysterical. I learned that if she doesn't get time alone she gets moody.

Whether you're vacationing in wonderfully exotic places with your grown children, camping with small children, spending a weekend on a houseboat, going to Grandma's, or just staying home in your own backyard and vegging out, time off for good behavior is vitally important. It's an old saw, but it's true that all work and no play makes Jane a dull girl.

If we tend toward work addiction, high expectations for ourselves, perfectionism, taking care of corporate business with a fervor—we need a vacation, a holiday, a break to regain our perspective. If you are a work addict, I have some amazing news for you: Work is not all there is to life!

Some other important news about learning how to rest is that the best use of vacation time is not in caring for the many toys our lifestyle has given us. There are lots of things that, if we're not careful, can begin to own us: travel trailers, cabins in the woods, recreational vehicles, big houses with big yards, horses, and other pets. There's nothing wrong with any of these things, except that sometimes they begin to require more of us in terms of work than the pleasure we get from them is worth. If that's happening to you, it's time to reevaluate your relationship to them. Maybe they should be sold.

I had often heard the phrase by Thoreau that says, "The mass of men lead lives of quiet desperation." He also said, "Most of the luxuries, and many of the so-called comforts, of life are not only not indispensable, but positive hindrances to the elevation of mankind."

Things have become so important to us that we sacrifice everything else to have them. We work long hours of overtime for more money to buy more things. Vacations are put off until we've acquired one more thing. "We really wanted to go to Hawaii, but not this year." Sigh. "We have to paint the house instead." And your children grow up and leave home, and you wonder where the time went.

For some of us, it takes as much discipline to take time off for rest and relaxation as it does for us to work. In fact, for some of us, the routine of work has a kind of built-in comfort that makes it easier than finding recreational pursuits.

WHY IS RECREATION IMPORTANT?

We all need to work hard and succeed at our jobs. Success is good for our self-esteem. But if there is nothing but work, we become confused. There has to be some emotional payoff to keep us working, to give us the courage to go on.

The Jamaica trip was that for me. After my internship, I had always wanted to go back. When I stepped onto Jamaican soil and found it changed and not so changed, I had an emotional payoff that made years of working and waiting worthwhile. In this uptight, stress-filled world, vacationing is not a luxury, it's a necessity!

It isn't always the luxury vacation that brings the richest payoff in emotional reward. Sometimes, it's a very simple vacation. I've spent many vacations in a tent, and because the life is so simple—pared down to the bare bones of existence, a place to lie down and some way to cook my food—I come away refreshed. (Although if it rains the whole time I'm camping, that's not so restful!)

As I'm writing this, I'm thinking of a little East Coast town I discovered at the end of the trip with my daughter. I loved that little town and did not have enough time to see it properly. It's near some of the best hiking trails in the East and not so far from some big cities. I'm going back there soon to rest, think, exercise, read, and enjoy the beauty of the place. That's a goal toward which to work. It's something that will help me focus my work this next year.

TRAVELING FOR THE FUN OF IT

We've established the fact that one of the rewards of hard work is time off. Now, we have to decide that at least once a year we will take time for nothing more than rest and recreation. How long that time should be depends on how tired you are, how long it's been since you've taken the last break, how long it takes you to recoup and regain perspective on life, how many funds are available, and a lot of other factors that only you know about.

I once was so tired that it took three weeks of a four-week vacation for me to begin to see that work is not everything there is to life. I had gone too long and become too tired, and it took a long time to rest. Don't let it happen to you.

WHAT SHOULD I SPEND ON RECREATION?

You should not spend what you don't have. The idea behind a vacation is to reduce stress. Spending money you don't have will only increase your stress level as you spend the next few months trying to pay off the vacation. It's a bit like paying for a car that has been wrecked or food that has already been eaten. It's not much fun.

Once you recognize that rest and recreation are important to your emotional health, to your general well-being, you will begin to regularly set aside money for recreation. And there are lots of vacations that don't cost too much.

Check your local library or bookstore for books about inexpensive travel and vacationing.

Several years ago I wrote a book called *Raising Kids on Purpose for the Fun of It*. That book is filled with ideas for family fun. In fact, I listed hundreds of ideas from *A* to *Z*. Here is a sampling:

- When you go to a new city, visit airports, go antiquing, see if there's an arboretum or a conservatory, learn about the architecture of the city. Visit art museums, observatories, beaches.
- Take a historical vacation and visit battlefields, old cemeteries, national monuments, Washington, D. C.
- Go to the beach, go berry picking or bird-watching.
- Go bicycling or caving.
- Fly a kite.
- Go fishing or hunting.
- Visit a glacier or go rock hunting.
- Watch glassmakers or potters.
- Take a hot-air balloon ride or go river rafting.
- Take a home tour, visit a hobby show.
- Visit a fire station or a lighthouse.
- Go to an outdoor concert or art show.
- See a play.
- Visit a theme park or see a sporting event.
- Hike to the top of a mountain or a waterfall.
- Go to a farm or a zoo.[1]

There are lots of wonderful, fun events everyone can enjoy. Watch weekend papers for more ideas in your vicinity. Start a file of ideas and clippings, organized by type of activity (river rafting, hiking, beaches, shopping malls) or by region or state. Make a list of the things you most want to do and start to do them. If you have children, focus on those things you especially want to do together while your children are at home with you. Time goes by all too quickly. If you are a single parent, search even more diligently for inexpensive vacation ideas or figure out ways to bring in more income for your trip. Older kids can earn money and help out. Don't delay life. Keep living, keep moving, keep doing. Remember, you've earned the right to time off.

Here's an example of a chart that your family could make and fill in with favorite activities, costs, equipment needed, and time required.

ACTIVITY	EQUIPMENT NEEDED	COST	TIME
CAMPING	Camping equipment; we have	$8 per night for campsite; $10 for gas	3 days minimum
BIKING	Bikes (rent)	$7 x 4 people = $28	I day

WHAT TO DO WHEN YOU CAN'T AFFORD TIME OR MONEY TO DO ANYTHING

Play games with your kids—or borrow some kids if you don't have any. See the suggested reading lists at the end of this chapter for some books with lots of ideas for games. Here are a few to get you started:

- Kick-the-can
- Duck, duck, goose
- Punch ball
- Hide-and-seek
- Statue
- Simon says
- Cat's cradle
- Jacks
- Monkey in the middle
- Red light, green light
- Freeze tag
- Red rover, red rover
- Capture the flag
- Stick ball
- Dodge ball
- Hopscotch
- Mother, may I?
- Jump rope
- Leapfrog

BEATING THE HIGH COST OF AIR TRAVEL

- Become a courier for large companies wanting to transport documents from one country to another. Some of these services pay all the airfare, and others pay most of it. After you get to a country, you're on your own for housing, transportation, and meals. Some agencies for air couriers are Halbart Express, 708-656-8189; Now Voyager, New York and Houston, 212-431-1616; Way-to-Go-Travel, Los Angeles and San Francisco, 213-466-1126; and Line Haul Services, Miami, 305-477-0651.

- Fly on a charter. Some have unbelievably low excursion rates and package deals.
- On some airlines you can still save money by flying at night.
- Several new airlines have sprung up that offer extremely low, no-frills fares. Some of these airlines do not fly as frequently as major airlines, and scheduling can be extremely difficult. It will take some planning ahead to make it work for you.
- If you have flexibility, join a last-minute travel club. These groups buy up unused or canceled tickets and sell them at a great discount — sometimes as much as one-third off. You just have to be ready to go within a few days' notice. Here are some of those clubs: Encore Short Notice, 800-638-8976; South Florida Cruises, 800-327-SHIP; Spur of the Moment Cruises, 800-343-1991.
- Look in the travel section of your Sunday paper for very small ads that promise tickets for less. They are legitimate. Here are a couple of well-known ticket discounters: Unitravel, 800-325-2222; Maharaja Travel, 800-223-6862.

- Travel off-season if possible. Airfares and hotels are much less expensive. The downside is that sometimes the tourist attractions are closed during off-season. But there is a time just after Labor Day and again just before Memorial Day when most tourist attractions will be open and rates will be down. They also happen to be times of good weather in most of the country.
- Become a frequent flyer of all the airlines. Special coupons are often issued to frequent flyers only. So in addition to racking up miles for free travel, you are also informed of specials—two flying for the price of one, reductions in airfare, hotels, and car rentals, etc.

MONEY-SAVING TIPS FOR GROUND TRANSPORTATION

- Be careful when leaving an airport and jumping into a taxi. In some cities (especially foreign cities) taxi fares vary widely. Ask the driver what the price to your destination will be before getting into the cab. If possible, take public transportation into the city and take a taxi from there.
- Use public transportation whenever possible. Many cities have mass transit subways that come right into the airport. Buses are cheap and take you right to your destination.
- See if the hotel where you are staying has limo service to the airport. Use it—it's free, but tip the driver.

USING RENTAL CARS

- Use coupons issued by your frequent flyer program to reduce costs.
- Shop around. Prices for rental cars vary greatly from company to company and location to location.
- Check weekly and weekend rates. Warning—if you turn in the car ahead of the scheduled time, you will probably have to pay a daily rate.
- Reserve ahead for the best rates. Sometimes reservations fill up quickly, and lower-priced cars are gone first.
- If you are going to be using rental cars frequently, make sure you have a provision for it on your personal automobile insurance to avoid paying rental car company insurance rates.
- Always return a rental car filled with gasoline. If you don't, they will fill it and charge you astronomical rates.
- Always return the car to the same place where you rented it to avoid drop charges, which can be substantial.

HOTELS

Surprisingly, inexpensive motel chains are not always the best bargain. Sometimes upscale chains run specials with unbelievable discounts. I recently stayed in a $350 per night hotel room in Vail, Colorado, for the supersaver price of $85. So shop around—and use toll-free numbers to do it.

Business hotels, such as Courtyard by Marriott, run specials during their low business-traffic times. Sometimes it is possible to stay for less than fifty dollars per night.

Great lodging bargains that are often overlooked are cheap, decent downtown hotels. These are not the highly advertised chain hotels but the privately owned older ones. Many of these have been refurbished to make them extremely comfortable and full of charm. Since they are leftovers from the days when businessmen traveled by train and needed accommodations close to the train stations, they are in the heart of the cities.

HOME EXCHANGES

Those who have exchanged homes for a vacation say it works and it's lots of fun. It can be done nationally or internationally. Most of those who exchange homes do so through a home-exchange club. Half the listings for one of the clubs were for homes in forty different foreign countries. Listings in the United States were mostly for second homes along the Atlantic or Pacific Ocean. (Some clubs have a membership fee.)

Here are a few home-exchange clubs:

Trading Homes International
P.O. Box 787
Hermosa Beach, CA 90254
1-800-877-8723

Affordable Travel Club, Inc.
6556 Snug Harbor Lane
Gig Harbor, WA 98335
206-858-2172

FOOD AND EATING OUT

Part of the fun of a vacation is eating out: eating things you don't normally eat in places that are new and exciting.

One of the problems of travel is eating too much—especially when traveling for pleasure. Ask yourself, Just how much do I need to eat, and what is my favorite meal of the day? It could be that you don't need three square meals a day.

Is breakfast your favorite meal? Many hotels have a wonderful brunch with as much food available as you will need for the entire day. Perhaps a sturdy breakfast a little later in the morning, no lunch, a snack in the afternoon, and dinner at a reasonable hour might be all you need.

Would fruit and cheese suffice for a lunchtime break? If economy is a factor, eat your largest meal at noon, when prices may be considerably less than at night.

I like to save some of my calorie intake for afternoon snack times when I am traveling for pleasure. I love English high tea. What an elegant, civilized idea! High tea is served between three and five in the afternoon. Many cities now have tea shops. Old hotels often have a teatime. It will take a little searching to find these tea shops, but they are well worth the search.

When traveling for fun, don't overlook the out-of-the-way ethnic eating places and tiny eateries off the main street. Most of them have home cooking that is superb. They are safe, they are clean, they are inexpensive—they just may not be very fancy. Be adventurous when it comes to food.

On one family vacation, I remember going into a drugstore for some film, somewhere out in North Dakota. I discovered the drugstore had an old-fashioned soda bar with a real marble-top counter. You were handed a glass and the mixing container, which meant you got about three times as much milk shake or malt as you would in most places. I went out to the car and brought everybody inside for a treat not to be forgotten.

If you are traveling internationally, be adventurous, but be careful. There isn't much that's worse than a bad case of the trots when you are on vacation. Usually, when traveling internationally I don't eat food on the street. There are no restrictions for such operations, and you are really taking chances. If possible, I also try to get a peek at the kitchens of indoor eating places. I just feel better knowing that the kitchen is clean.

CAMPING AS A WAY OF AFFORDING A TRIP

I'm a strong advocate of camping as a way for families to take wonderful, inexpensive vacations. Once the initial investment of equipment is made (and this can often be purchased secondhand), there is only the gas to get where you are going and the campground fees, usually under ten dollars per campsite.

If you plan ahead and make reservations, you can hardly call camping roughing it. You can take hot showers, swim in heated pools, use the campground laundromat, sit in a hot tub, play video games, go to campfire presentations given by naturalists, and purchase food at the campground store. This kind of camping can put you at the heart of some of the most interesting areas of the country. There are campsites near Disneyland, Mount St. Helens, Niagara Falls, and every other attraction in the country.

Last year on a trip to Yellowstone, my friend and I stopped at a commercial campground. It was late when we got in, but we went over to the clubhouse and climbed into the hot tub. It was wonderful to sit soaking up the heat, looking up at the stars, and listening to the coyotes howl and the frogs croak. We were in the heart of the Tetons. It was an inexpensive way to be where we wanted to be, right on the border of Yellowstone Park.

Keep camping simple and to the basics. Decide whether you want to cook or just want to sleep in the tent or RV. If you do not cook, you increase the expense but you decrease the amount of equipment you need to take.

Whatever you do, get good sleeping bags and good pads to sleep on. I personally don't like air mattresses; they always lose air. I prefer a two-inch foam pad. Get an adequate-sized tent and practice setting it up. Learn how to trench the ground around the tent and why it's important. Assign tasks to different members of the family that they do every time you arrive at a campground.

When doing full-scale camping with my family, I always made breakfast and lunch at the same time. Lunch went into a cooler (or backpack, if we were hiking). Meals were planned well ahead of time, and all food was removed from boxes and put in resealable plastic bags with the instructions enclosed. This conserved space.

I also made small pillows and pillowcases of a dark print material that would not show the soil too quickly. The cases had handles sewn on so they could be carried onto an airplane over one's arm.

As in so many things about life, our attitude about camping can be good or bad, happy or miserable — it's up to us. For inexpensive family vacations, I think camping needs to be revisited.

BIG VACATIONS VERSUS MINIVACATIONS

A trend in recent years is the minivacation. Instead of a two-week trek with the kids stuffed in the backseat of a station wagon, families are opting for two- and three-day trips close to home.

The idea has some advantages. Less time is spent traveling. That saves time and money. There is less weariness on everyone's part. More time is spent resting. The breaks come more frequently so that family members can rest more often throughout the year.

The disadvantages are that often it takes more than three or four days to even begin to relax. Extended vacations give us time enough to get tired of being on vacation and ready to get back to work.

Maybe the real answer is to vary the vacation time from year to year. Some years, take an extended vacation to allow everyone to thoroughly rest. Other years, take several minivacations and stay close to home.

Whatever choice you make, the important thing is to make the choice to take time off for rest. None of us is indispensable at work — we just think we are. We have little to give from the empty, burned-out shells we become when we refuse to rest. Leisure is an excellent use of our time. We've earned it. We need it.

SUGGESTED READING FOR WOMEN TRAVELING ALONE

Eleanor Berman, *Traveling on Your Own* (New York: Crown, 1990).

SUGGESTED READING FOR FAMILY TRAVEL

Evelyn Kaye, *Family Travel: Terrific New Vacations for Today's Families* (Boulder: Blue Penguin, 1993).

Sanford Portnoy and Joan Portnoy, *How to Take Great Trips with Your Kids* (Boston: Harvard Common, 1984).

Gwen Weising, *Raising Kids on Purpose for the Fun of It* (Grand Rapids: Baker, 1989).

Finding Time for Family Fun (Grand Rapids: Baker, 1991).

Finding Dollars for Family Fun: Creating Home Memories on a Budget (Grand Rapids: Baker, 1993).

SUGGESTED READING FOR ECONOMY TRAVEL

Linda Bowman, *How to Fly for Free* (Chicago: Probus, 1991).

Theodore Fischer, *Cheap/Smart Travel* (New York: M. Evans, 1987).

Walter Weintz and Caroline Weintz, *The Discount Guide for Travelers over 55* (New York: NAL-Dutton, 1985).

SUGGESTED READING FOR VACATIONS THAT ARE DIFFERENT

Pat Dickerman, *Farm, Ranch, and Country Vacations* (Newfoundland, N.J.: Farm, Ranch and Country Vacations Publ., 1989).

Fodor's Healthy Escapes: Spas, Fitness Resorts, Cruises (New York: Fodor's Travel, 1993).

T.J. "Tex" Hill, *Adventure Traveling: Where the Packaged Tours Won't Take You* (Bedford, Mass.: Mills and Sanderson, 1986).

Evelyn Kaye, *Travel and Learn: The New Guide to Educational Travel* (Boulder: Blue Penguin, 1992).

Bill McMillon, *Volunteer Vacations: Short-Term Adventures That Will Benefit You and Others* (Chicago: Chicago Review, 1993).

Carol Spivack and Richard A. Weinstock, *Best Festivals of North America: A Performing Arts Guide* (Ventura, Calif.: Printwheel, 1989).

SUGGESTED READING FOR FAMILY GAMES

Fred Ferretti, *The Great American Book of Sidewalk, Stoop, Dirt, Curb and Alley Games* (New York: Workman, 1975).

Darwin A. Hindman, *Kick-the-Can and Over 800 Other Active Games and Sports* (New York: Prentice Hall, 1978).

Phil Wiswell, *Kids' Games: Traditional Indoor and Outdoor Activities for Children of All Ages* (New York: Doubleday, 1987).

SUGGESTED GENERAL READING

Stephen A. Shapiro, *Time Off: A Psychological Guide to Vacations* (Garden City, N.Y.: Anchor, 1978).

Gwen Ellis can be contacted
for speaking engagements

c/o Tyndale House Publishers
P.O. Box 80
Wheaton, IL 60189-0080

NOTES

Chapter 1: The Things That Try My Soul

1. Joni Balter, "Women and Work," *Seattle Times*, 25 April 1991, E1.
2. Balter, "Women and Work."
3. Sybil Stanton, *The Twenty-Five-Hour Woman: The Guilt-Free Way to Manage Your Time* (New York: Bantam, 1990), 225.

Chapter 2: It Takes Planning

1. Tom Heymann, *In An Average Lifetime* (New York: Fawcett, 1991).
2. Ralph Keyes, "Do You Have the Time?" *Parade*, 16 February 1992, 22–24.
3. J. B. Schor, *The Overworked American: The Unexpected Decline of Leisure* (New York: Basic Books, 1991), 17ff.
4. Robert J. Samuelson, "Technology in Reverse," *Newsweek*, 20 July 1992, 45.
5. Adapted from Keyes, "Have the Time?"

Chapter 3: Getting Help

1. Charles Whited, "Widening Rift between Sexes Hurts Us All," *Denver Post*.
2. Remember that some things that are bartered are considered taxable by the IRS. If you have any questions, consult with an accountant or an IRS office.

Chapter 4: The Married Working Woman

1. "Workforce: Year 2000," *Marketing to Women* 5, no. 3 (December 1991): 14.
2. Lynn Smith and Bob Sipchen, "Two-Career Family Dilemma: Balancing Work and Home," *Los Angeles Times*, 12 August 1990, A1.
3. Catherine Johnson, "Secrets of Lasting Love" (condensed from *Lucky in Love*), *Reader's Digest*, May 1992, 141–144.

4. Smith and Sipchen, "Two-Career Family."

5. Rosalind C. Barnett and Caryl Rivers, "The Myth of the Miserable Working Woman," *Working Woman*, February 1992, 62–65.

6. Johnson, "Lasting Love."

7. "Management," *Marketing to Women* 5, no. 3 (December 1991): 14.

8. Smith and Sipchen, "Two-Career Family."

Chapter 5: The Single Working Woman

1. Patricia Braus, "Sex and the Single Shopper," *American Demographics*, November 1993, 34.

2. Sandra Sanchez, "Equality of Sexes? Give It 1,000 Years," *USA Today*, 1993, A1.

3. Debbie Warhola, "Programs Let Employees Give of Their Time," *Gazette Telegraph*, 14 February 1993, E1.

Chapter 6: The Primary Caregiver

1. NBC news, 26 May 1994.

2. Michael Ryan, "Who's Taking Care of the Children?" *Parade*, 30 August 1992, 4.

3. Anne Mitchell with Diane Gage, "Day Care in the '90s," *Good Housekeeping*, September 1992, 174.

4. Sally Wendkos Olds, *The Working Parents Survival Guide* (Rocklin, Calif.: Prima Publishing and Communications, 1989), 67.

5. Susan Krafft, "Mom Says She's Doing Better," *American Demographics*, February 1993, 16.

6. Elys A. McLean, "USA Snapshorts," *USA Today*, based on information from Bureau of Labor Statistics, 1992.

7. Catherine Wilson, "Family Leave," *Gazette Telegraph*, 27 May 1992, G1.

8. Mitchell, "Day Care."

9. Adapted from Mitchell, "Day Care."

10. Helen L. Swan and Victoria Houston, *Alone after School* (New York: Prentice-Hall, 1985), vii.

11. Editorial, "Caregivers Need to Find Time for Themselves," *USA Today*, 19 April 1989, 5D.

Chapter 7: The Harried Cook

1. Francine Hermelin, "The Food-Stress Link," *Working Woman*, May 1993, 92.

2. Ibid.

3. Mimi Wilson and Mary Beth Lagerborg, *Once-a-Month Cooking* (Colorado Springs: Focus on the Family, 1992).

4. For more time- and money-saving ideas, see two of my other books. They are: *Finding Time for Family Fun* and *Finding Dollars for Family Fun* (Grand Rapids: Baker).

Chapter 8: Finding the Perfect Job

1. For more information on this evaluation process, see Richard Earle and David Imrie, *Your Vitality Quotient: The Clinically Proven Program That Can Reduce Your Body Age and Increase Your Zest for Life* (New York: Warner, 1990).

Chapter 9: Don't Just Hang in There!

1. Marsha Sinetar, *Do What You Love, the Money Will Follow: Discovering Your Right Livelihood* (New York: Dell, 1989), 1.

2. Ellie Winninghoff, "Crashing the Glass Ceiling," *Entrepreneurial Woman*, March/April 1990, 66.

Chapter 10: Handling Tough Job Situations

1. Susan Webb, *Step Forward* (New York: Mastermedia, 1991), 25–26.

2. Ronni Sandroff, "Sexual Harassment, the Inside Story," *Working Woman*, June 1992, 47–51.

3. Glynis M. Breakwell, *The Quiet Rebel* (New York: Grove Press, Inc., 1985), 94.

Chapter 11: Watch Out for the Danger Zone

1. Bryan E. Robinson, *Work Addiction* (Deerfield Beach, Fla.: Health Communications, Inc., 1989), 34. Used with permission.

2. Robinson, *Work Addiction*, 36–38.

3. Diane Fassel, *Working Ourselves to Death: The High Cost of Work Addiction and the Rewards of Recovery* (San Francisco: HarperCollins, 1990), 57–58.

4. Ellen Sue Stern, *The Indispensable Woman* (New York: Bantam, 1988), 15.

Chapter 12: Growing Spiritually

1. Joan Wilson, "He's Calling You Now," *Union Life*.

2. Sinetar, *Do What You Love*, 208.

3. Gabriele Rico, *Pain and Possibility* (Los Angeles: Jeremy P. Tarcher, Inc., 1991), ix.

4. Ibid., x.

Chapter 13: Healthy Living

1. Jeanine Barone, "Making Health a Family Affair," *Working Woman*, November 1989, 179.

2. Gayle Sato, "Shape Up," *Entrepreneurial Woman*, March/April 1990, 99.

3. Harriet B. Braiker, "Does Superwoman Have It the Worst?" *Working Woman*, August 1988, 65.

Chapter 14: Learning to Play

1. Gwen Weising, *Raising Kids on Purpose for the Fun of It* (Grand Rapids: Baker, 1989). See pages 167–190 for *A* to *Z* index.

Discover These Sources of Inspiration for the Lifestyles of Today's Women:

THE CHRISTIAN WORKING MOTHER'S HANDBOOK
Advice from a mother's personal experience on organization, private time, career goals, and more.
Jayne Garrision 0-8423-0258-1

THE DESIRES OF A WOMAN'S HEART
An acclaimed spokeswoman encourages women to pursue traditional Christian values often rejected in today's society.
Beverly LaHaye 0-8423-7945-2

FRAN & JESUS ON THE JOB
Humorous, encouraging vignettes that depict a woman's ability to weather daily problems with Jesus as her companion.
Mary S. Whelchel 0-8423-1226-9

THE FRAZZLED MOTHER'S GUIDE TO INNER PEACE
Addresses the nonstop responsibilities of a new mother with encouragement and support from God's Word.
Pat Baker 0-8423-0926-8